DO YOU FEEL CALLED BY GOD?

Rethinking the call to ministry

MICHAEL BENNETT

CONTENTS

WHY I WROTE THIS BOOK

I have written this book from a very personal perspective. It is not meant to be some kind of autobiography, but I do want to convey some of the struggles I went through in my early life as a Christian believer, and especially the struggles I had with the often-heard expression, "I feel God is calling me into the ministry". The content of this book has not been written in an academic ivory tower in order to add yet one more tome to the voluminous titles that choke our Christian bookstores. Most of the topics I deal with here concern struggles I have personally experienced in trying to understand the sacred Scriptures and the faith called evangelical Christianity.

The object of this book is to attempt to help people who are seeking the guidance of God in their lives, and who may particularly be considering full-time Christian ministry. What does the Bible actually teach about the call of God, in both the Old and New Testaments? Should we expect to experience dramatic and overt signs such as the Israelites witnessed in the olden days? Should we actually hear the voice of God, or see a moving finger writing on the wall? Is there any such thing as 'the call of God'? My desire is to set down the results of my own research over many years, and to be helpful.

In chapters 3 and 4, I examine the use of the word 'call' and the recorded examples of God having called people throughout the pages of first the Old Testament and then the New Testament. My studies in this area have led me to attempt a detailed analysis of the Greek verb *kalein*, 'to call', and its cognates within the Greek New Testament. What I have discovered is a word so rich, so varied in its meaning, that (as I comment later in the book) it is hard to see how the New Testament could have been composed without it! 'Call' is used in vital connection with just about every phase of Christian experience, from gospel proclamation to regeneration to faith to holiness. The very word 'church' is a noun cognate of *kalein*. I have discovered that 'call' is used more than 300 times within the pages of the New Testament, and with at least 11 separate meanings. You can find the results of this examination in chapter 5.

Out of this detailed examination I have arrived at two conclusions in regard to the important subject of the 'call of God', conclusions that I think can fairly be described as radical within the context of everyday evangelical piety today. The rest of this book explains the process by which these conclusions have been reached. The conclusions are:

1. The often-heard and almost universally accepted expression "I feel God is calling me" is totally foreign to the revealed content of both the Old and New Testaments of the Bible. The continued use of this unscriptural pietistic language may be having negative consequences for churches, missionary societies and other Christian organizations in the choosing and training of future leaders.

2. *Without denying in any way God's ability to call people into ministry by overt and supernatural signs*, it is argued here that this is not usually God's method today. The motivation to serve the Lord, particularly in what is termed full-time ministry, is *a human desire* to do so, and not a *felt call*.

However, this human desire, which must spring from one's love for Jesus and the gospel and genuine compassion for people, is not sufficient or valid in itself: it must be *rightly motivated and rightly tested.*

The remainder of this book argues this second conclusion, but particular attention is given to it in chapter 10, aptly titled 'A human desire'. If you are one of those people who like to read the ending of a detective novel at the beginning, you may choose to read chapter 10 now and then decide whether you want to read the rest of the book.

I hope you will not think me big-headed if I say that I wish I had had a book like this when I started out. It would have short-circuited a lot of time and heartache.

one

A MOUSE CALLED SPIRIT

The long-fringed lampshade, Western movie style, hung low over the green baize tablecloth. A group of dark-clothed, sober-faced men sat staring at me as I waited apprehensively for their enquiries to begin. In the dim light I could see collars of white turned towards me. In a moment of madness I imagined that one of them might actually produce a pack of cards and begin to deal. Finally, the question came that I knew must come, and for which I had no answer that would satisfy them: "And why do you feel God is calling you into the ministry?" Actually, that was the second time I had heard the same question within the space of a few minutes. The first time it had come from my own lips on the other side of the old panelled door just before I had been called in.

I had been sitting in a kind of vestibule with another young man of about my own age as we nervously waited for our turn to be interviewed. We were applying to enter the local theological college of our church denomination with the possible long-term result of going into full-time ministry, though I was by no means convinced at this stage that that was where I wanted to finish up.

I had not met this young man before and, as far as I know, I have not again since. But as we fell into rather strained conversation, awaiting our turn to face a panel of our church leaders, I was somewhat surprised by the direction in which our conversation went. He began to tell me about his girlfriend, and then began to relate some of the exploits he and she got up to in the back seat of his car at the drive-in movies. At that time, drive-in movies were a novelty in our town (before television killed most of them off) and had the reputation of being modern-day 'lovers' lanes'.

Now it occurred to me that in view of the occasion, this was a rather bizarre conversation. We were sitting there waiting to be asked why we wanted to enter theological college, and why we considered we might be fit and suited to enter the ministry of the sacred gospel. It seemed surreal. I knew that at any moment I was about to face the selection panel, and I also sensed that they were going to ask me the question for which I knew I had no ready or satisfactory answer, so I decided to put the same question to my nervous colleague: "Why do you feel God is calling you into the ministry?"

The answer that came back, I felt, was even more bizarre than the previous conversation, and my immediate reaction was to say to myself, "There must be a better reason than that!" I will come back to his reply in the next chapter. But eventually that day I did sit before the selection committee, and inevitably that question was asked of me, and I had to reply honestly, "I'm sorry, I do not feel called to the ministry. I would, however, like to study at the college, and I am open to anything the Lord may call me to in the future; but I cannot truthfully say at the moment that I do feel called."

These conversations started me on a drawn-out, painful, and sometimes perplexing quest to discover the answer to this seemingly pivotal question. They also led, in time, to deeper questions such as, "What do we mean by the call of God?" and

"What does the Bible teach about the call of God?" I will come back to these questions later, but first I need to sketch in briefly the chain of events that led me to this turning point in my life.

Early days

I grew up in Australia at a time when it was considered right and proper for parents to send their children to Sunday School at the local church. Neither of my parents was a believer or religious, but in those days you could be considered a negligent parent if you did not encourage your children in this direction. I think my parents' motive was their hope that I might pick up some morals that would help me through my later life. If they had known then that it would be an important link in a chain of events that would eventually lead me into full-time Christian ministry, I am fairly sure they would immediately have stopped me from going!

So while my parents sat up in bed with the Sunday morning papers, my siblings and I were sent off to the local Anglican church for Christian instruction. I was not all that interested and would get out of going as often as I could, but over a number of years I picked up a good smattering of Bible stories. However, probably because of the hit-and-miss nature of my unwilling attendance, these stories were all jumbled together with no coherent order, and I would have sympathized with the question a girl once asked in a religious education class, "Miss, did Moses come to Australia before Captain Cook, or after?"[1]

When I was too old to attend children's Sunday School I

1. It may come as a surprise to know what Sunday was like in those not-so-distant days. There was no television and no Sunday sport. No shop or picture theatre would dare to open its doors to the public on a Sunday. In fact, the most exciting pastimes available to many people on that day of the week were going to church or Sunday School, having a bush picnic with your relatives and friends, and listening to the radio at night.

went through something called 'Confirmation', which I took to be graduation, and promptly left off having any meaningful contact with the church. I would not return in any serious manner for more than ten years. The minister who prepared me for Confirmation, however, used an illustration of humanity that has remained with me ever since. If you rub mud on a wall, he told us, and then paint over it, for a while it will look all right. But after some time the paint will crack and peel and the muck underneath will begin to reveal itself. Somewhere deep in my heart I knew this was true. Although I liked to project a nice scrubbed-up middle-class appearance, and considered myself (wrongly) to be the moral equal (and even superior) of my peers, I was beginning to experience a taste of human depravity in my unseen moments.

School days

My father, being a medical doctor, had the funds to send me to a local church school from an early age. I was there for nine years and it was a very positive experience, though I enjoyed the sport and companionship much more than either the study or the spiritual side of school life.

In fact, in my last year, when we in our final grade were all meant to be the responsible school prefects and leaders, my class had the dubious distinction of driving one of the local church ministers out of the school forever. He would come in once a week to try to give us spiritual instruction, and our combined object was to destroy every lesson he attempted to present. He must have dreaded the day of the week on which we would torment him.

During one of these disrupted lessons, the minister gave out a sheet of paper with some notes on it. We students were continuing with our normal rubbishing behaviour ("Oh, sir, you've printed it upside down"; "No intelligent person could believe this, sir"; and similar comments) when one of the students turned around, held up the paper and said, "The answer is on the sheet, guys!" I was thunderstruck. John, the speaker, was on the minister's side! And John wasn't a nerd: he was captain of a premiership-winning cricket team! It was a small but courageous stand, and made a lasting impression on me.[2]

Eventually, in the middle of another disastrous lesson one day, the tormented minister shut his books and announced, "I'm sorry boys, but you are unteachable!" With that, he left the school and never came back. I can still remember him walking down the school driveway, head down, probably believing that he had totally failed his Lord. We did not mind; we had achieved our objective. The only sorrow from our perspective was that we forfeited what we considered to be a free period, as this was subsequently replaced with a normal lesson. On reflection, with the benefit of believer's hindsight, our behaviour was extreme and not a little demonic. The paint was peeling off and the muddy reality was on show. I am now ashamed of my own participation in this episode. The school now has full-time chaplains and I believe the situation is much improved, with a strong group of Christian students attending the school.

After leaving school I had a number of false starts, which I am sure cost my father a sizeable amount of hair, but I finally settled on architecture as the direction I wanted my life to take. It was possible then to study the course for six years either full-time at university or part-time at a technical college, and as I had lost a university scholarship as the result of one of my false

2. Some years later when I was in full-time ministry, John's sister attended our church. She mentioned this to John, whose reply was, "I remember a Michael Bennett from school, but it couldn't possibly be *that* Michael Bennett!"

starts, my father and I chose the latter. This meant working in an architect's office during the day and then going off to evening lectures. But by the fifth year of my studies the Hound of Heaven was on the loose.[3]

"There must be more to life!"

We have all heard stories of people who have become believing Christians because some disaster has come into life. A loved one has died; a terrible illness has struck; a marriage has fallen apart; financial ruin has occurred. One of the most famous of such stories is that of the American politician Chuck Colson, who was one of the closest advisers to the President of the United States. He had easy access to the then most powerful man in the world, Richard Nixon. But when the scandal called Watergate was uncovered, Nixon was forced to resign as President, and Colson and several of the other White House aides found themselves disgraced and in prison. In that context, Colson came to genuine repentance and faith in Christ, largely through reading CS Lewis's book *Mere Christianity*. Stories like this are not uncommon. Tragedy comes into a person's life, so the person comes to find a new beginning in Christ.

However, in my own case it was the very opposite. I became a Christian because everything in my life was going too well. Let me take you back to a period of about three months during my fifth year of studies, when I was 24 years old. For this three-month period, everything in my life was incredibly rosy. At the

....

3. 'The Hound of Heaven' is a Victorian poem by Francis Thompson (1859-1907). Born in a devout Catholic family, Thompson graduated in medicine but became an opium addict and vagrant. He was later rescued by a kind prostitute and Christian friends. His poem, much admired by Tolkien and Chesterton, is said to have partly inspired *The Screwtape Letters* by CS Lewis. It pictures a prodigal being relentlessly pursued by a loving God. The Victorian prose makes for hard reading today.

time I was playing rugby, which I loved, for one of the top local teams. I was eventually promoted to the first-grade senior team. During this period we won eight games in a row, which must still be something of a club record, and we were placed at the top of the rugby competition in our city. Although it was not usual for rugby matches to be televised, on one particular Saturday afternoon the cameras turned up to broadcast our game. We had a big win and I had one of my best games ever, scoring two tries that secured the match for us. The local newspaper used to take votes for the best and fairest player in each round of the competition and, to my surprise, there was my name. Some of my teammates reckoned I only played at my best when the cameras were rolling!

At the same time I was going out with a lovely girl with long blonde hair, and our tastes were very similar in terms of music, art, morals and life. She endured rugby! I was young and single with my own car and plenty of money with which to enjoy life. At work I was beginning to be given responsibility and allowed to take building projects from the first interview with the client right through to construction and completion, with little supervision from the firm's partners. Although I was never a brilliant student, I discovered later that I was one of only two students up to that time at the technical college who had completed the six-year architectural course without ever failing a subject and having to repeat. In another area, also, life in the Michael Bennett garden was just fine. I belonged to a painting group called the Contemporary Art Society and entered works into their exhibitions. During this rosy period one of my works was mentioned favourably in the papers, and someone even offered to buy one of my paintings!

I hope you will not think I am being boastful in relating all this. I just want to make the point that for one short period of my life, about three months, nearly everything was as good as it could be—as someone might crassly say today, "Life doesn't get any better than this!"

But I felt empty and miserable.

Walking to work one morning I recall saying to myself, "There must be more to life than I have discovered so far. I have all these things that the world tells me are to be desired and strived for, things that make life full and meaningful. Why do I feel so dissatisfied?"

A long and painful quest

For some unexplained reason, I felt the answer might lie in religion, so I began to undertake a preliminary examination of the great religions of the world. Christianity was the only faith I had ever known, so I looked into the other major alternatives. I bought books on Hinduism, Buddhism, Islam, Humanism and others. I read the works of Confucius. But still the nagging emptiness persisted. These all seemed to be conduits of man-made values and rules, laws and religious regulations. By this time the cracking paint was really beginning to fall away from the muck, and I was having to face the uncomfortable reality that I was not the superior moral being I had kidded myself into believing I was. I could not see how doing a few half-hearted religious practices would impress God if they did not impress me. Would my empty void really be filled by saying a few prayers when in trouble, undertaking fasts or joining pilgrimages? Was God so cheap that he could be bought off by an imperfect display of external religion?

At this time my rosy world began to fall apart. I was dropped from the top grade rugby side, there was a messy break-up with my girlfriend and, worst of all, my parents' marriage was beginning to disintegrate as a third party entered the equation.

Not knowing where to turn next, I considered that I should give Christianity another go—the faith that I had rejected, or rather neglected, since my early teens. I bought myself a modern translation of the New Testament and began to read it with some genuine interest for the first time ever. I began to attend a local church in the suburb where we lived. But immediately a series of doubts began to plague me.

The first was easily disposed of. I asked myself, "How do we know such a person as Jesus Christ ever existed? How do we know that the whole story about Jesus is not some fictitious invention, some kind of elaborate hoax that has somehow been inflicted on the world for whatever reason?"

I soon discovered, however, that three secular historians who lived during roughly the same period as Jesus mention him in their writings. These historians—Josephus, Tacitus and Suetonius—were not Christians, and in some cases were very hostile to the new religion. They were totally independent writers, with no reason to promote Christianity. Yet if you put their records together, it can be shown beyond reasonable doubt that a man called Jesus lived in Judea at the time recorded in the Bible, that he was put to death by Pontius Pilate in about 33 AD, and that his followers believed him to have risen from the dead.

But then, I reasoned, how do we know the story of Jesus has not been exaggerated and embellished, bearing little resemblance to the real happenings? There may have been a good man—perhaps even a prophet—called Jesus who did live at that time, but perhaps over time his life and teachings have been deliberately corrupted. After all, we have seen in our times the extent to which Hollywood film producers are masters of this craft!

There was another, similar question that had to be dealt with. It was the old 'Chinese whispers' argument. The gospels, with the rest of the New Testament, have been handed down over a period of some 2000 years. These writings have been copied and re-copied, and dozens of translations into English alone have been completed. How do we know that the text has not been altered during this process— a little here, a little there, until the final product bears little resemblance to the original?

I spent many hours in bookshops and libraries seeking to understand the documentary evidence for the transmission of the Bible, and especially the gospels, upon which virtually our whole knowledge of the life of Jesus depends. I found the evidence to be very impressive. A small army of textual scholars is constantly working on a rich supply of early New Testament manuscripts, and I became convinced that the New Testament we hold in our hands today is, for all practical purposes, a faithful record of the originals.[4]

Yet I found I still could not believe.

Next I began to look into the discipline of archaeology. Have those who specialize in digging up the past unearthed believable confirmation of the biblical record? There have been some impressive discoveries. The existence of King Belshazzar, mentioned in the Old Testament book of Daniel, was greatly doubted by secular scholars, as there was no mention of his existence in the Babylonian record. There seemed to have been no place available for him in the list of the kings of Babylon, which was believed to be a complete list. However, a more recent archaeological find has confirmed Belshazzar's existence, and also that he was co-regent with another king, Nabonidas, at the time of Babylon's demise.

One of the prized possessions in my personal library is the

4. Plenty of information on this subject is available through Christian bookshops. At that time I found FF Bruce's small book *The New Testament Documents: Are they Reliable?* extremely useful, and I believe it is still in print.

famous tome by Sir William Ramsay dated 1896 entitled *St Paul the Traveller and the Roman Citizen*. In it, Ramsay describes his early historical scepticism concerning the New Testament book 'The Acts of the Apostles'. Ramsay initially considered Acts to be a largely untrustworthy record, essentially a fiction written a considerable time later than the writings of the apostles. The writer's object, he believed, was to provide some pious stories about the doings of the early leaders of the Christian church, legends composed at a significantly later period, and also to support a supposed 'Paul versus Jesus' faction in the early church. Ramsay spent a considerable portion of his life comparing the historical, geographical and cultural details found in Acts against the records we possess concerning life in the Roman Empire at the time of Jesus and the apostles. The result of this intensive investigation was a total reversal of his views. In section 1 of the opening chapter, entitled 'Trustworthiness', Ramsay states:

> There is… [in Acts] the historical work of the highest order, in which a writer commands excellent means of knowledge either through personal acquaintance or through access to original authorities…[5]

Ramsay goes on to explain one of his reasons for "placing the author of Acts among the historians of the first rank":[6]

> It was gradually borne in upon me that in various details the narrative showed marvellous truth.[7]

Now there is a sting in the tail here that may not be obvious. There is a large body of scholarly agreement that both Acts and

5. WM Ramsay, *St Paul the Traveller and the Roman Citizen*, GP Putnam's Sons, New York, 1896, p. 2.
6. Ramsay, p. 4.
7. Ramsay, p. 8.

the Gospel of Luke were written by the same hand—that of the physician Luke, Paul's regular travelling companion. If so, it is reasonable to argue that if Acts can be found to be historically trustworthy, and its author proven to be a historian of the highest integrity, then the same may be said about the Gospel of Luke. If this is so, then it is reasonable to hold that the story of Jesus in Luke is also likely to be a reliable record.

Vast tracts of the Bible are not, or cannot be, confirmed by archaeology. For instance, for obvious reasons no archaeological record can ever be found for the account that Jesus walked on water. But archaeology does allow us to dip into the historical record at various points to test its trustworthiness, not unlike the time-to-time quality control exercised in a factory. Once again, I found this process, even with all its inherent limitations, to be impressive.

Yet still I found I simply could not believe!

By this stage I was in considerable despair. I had collected a small mountain of material concerning the trustworthiness of the Jesus record (and I was later to discover there was not much I had missed), and yet still this tenacious unbelief remained.

A mouse called Spirit

A little mouse had begun his work, however. Let me picture my stubborn unbelief as being like a large pile of wheat, and the Holy Spirit as a small hungry mouse. Bit by bit, at an agonizingly slow pace, this mouse began to eat his way through the pile. I desperately wanted to find meaning and purpose for my life, and by now I was seeing the cross of Jesus as the stark difference between Christianity and all other religions. I also perceived the cross as the answer to the peeling paint, which was more and more exposing my truly depraved nature, but I found I could not believe. How could I place all my faith in—

and be 100 percent committed to—a person for whom there was incomplete (if impressive) evidence as to his true significance? (Apart from the gospels, whose writers, I reasoned, obviously wished to promote his cause.)

Metamorphosis

It took that slow, steady mouse about 18 months to complete his tedious work. Gradually, painfully, I knew not how, the pile of unbelief was disappearing and faith was being born. There was no dramatic heavenly thunderclap; no band struck up; but while sitting alone in church late one night, I found myself saying, "I do not want to live my life any longer without Jesus". A metamorphosis was taking place. The grub was dying and the butterfly was struggling to emerge. Now that I know a bit more Christian theology, I would say that what was happening to me at that time was called spiritual 'regeneration' or new birth by the inward work of the Holy Spirit; but I did not know that then. All I knew was that, like the man who was blind from birth in John's Gospel, "though I was blind, now I [could] see" (John 9:25).

Decision time

By this stage I was nearing the end of my six years of architectural study and needed to make a decision about life after graduation. I enjoyed the profession of architecture very much and probably could have continued to work for the firm that employed me. But I desperately wanted to understand the Bible more fully. Apart from Sunday School, my Christian instruction had been haphazard and sketchy at best. I felt I understood the gospels reasonably well, but the epistles and the Old Testament remained largely puzzling mysteries.

Much to my parents' dismay, I decided to apply for entry to

a local theological college. My mother would later say to her friends that it was "a waste of a damn fine architect", but from my perspective she was mistaken on two counts: it was not a waste; and I was not a damn fine architect.

two

"I FEEL GOD IS CALLING ME"

The leaves of the South American looking plant were long, straight, stiff and tipped with a sharp iron-like point. I now know these plants are called yuccas. I stood there, irresolute, trying to calculate whether I could jump over this plant while dressed in something resembling a long black nightgown without doing myself some permanent damage. After all, I was young and in reasonable trim. I hesitated on the brink, and then decided...

As I mentioned in the previous chapter, before I could be allowed to enter college to study the Bible and theology, I was required to appear before a selection committee; and as I sat nervously in a small room with another candidate, waiting to be interviewed, I asked the other young man the question that was troubling me, and which I was sure was going to be asked of me on the other side of the door.

"Why do you feel God is calling you into the ministry?" I enquired.

As I said before, his reply rather surprised me.

"Recently," he answered, "the minister of my church was going to be away on holidays, and he asked me whether I would lead one of the church services in his absence. I had never done this before, but I agreed to help. When I entered the church to begin the service, the whole congregation stood up. Now, no-one had ever stood up for me before, and I enjoyed this so much that I decided I would like to go into the ministry full-time!"[1]

My immediate unspoken reaction was to think, "There must be a better reason than that!" I felt in my bones that there had to be a worthier motivation for considering full-time ministry, but I could not think what it might be. I certainly felt no such inner conviction.

Despite my unsatisfactory interview, I was accepted by the selection committee, and the beginning of my 26th year saw me entering the college complete with empty notebooks, new pens and a pile of newly purchased books with daunting titles like *A New Eusebius*. There were about 38 other students, spread over three years of study.

The brewery and Holy Communion

Almost immediately a new set of problems began to emerge for me. The college I attended would have then described its theological emphasis as 'Liberal Catholic', and I think it still would. At one level the 'Catholic' part meant that the college, although Anglican, had a strong Roman Catholic flavour to it. The campus had something of a monastic feel. For instance, we were officially allowed to leave the college for only a few hours on Sunday afternoons. Most days we were required to dress in long black cassocks. There was a beautiful old stone chapel, which was probably built by convicts in the earlier colonial days of Australia. As an architect I found it and many of the campus buildings very attractive. The chapel was the centre of our communal life and we regularly had three or four

....

1. Some may be surprised to discover that in many congregations people used to stand when the minister or pastor entered. I am not advocating the return of this custom!

services a day there, often involving a medieval style of chanting called plainsong. The first service of the day was always Holy Communion, which was held before breakfast. Unfortunately, the college was built right next to one of the biggest breweries in Australia, and they usually started their daily brew at about the same time. The combination of an empty stomach and the strong hops odour was an interesting experience when the wind blew in our direction!

As one entered the chapel there was a large life-sized crucifix outside the door and holy water just inside. Religious pictures adorned the walls and our services involved candles, plainsong chanting, colourful robes and the frequent use of incense. As Easter approached, the frequency of these services increased. On one particular day we went through all seven services used by monks of the Benedictine monasteries in the Middle Ages, as well as our regular church services. We were in the chapel about ten times that day.

On the Thursday of Easter week (called Maundy Thursday in the church calendar), we were informed that we were to have a special service in the chapel called 'The Fleeing of the Chapel'. Our Christian faith was to be expressed in drama, we were told, and in this service we were to re-enact physically the moment in the gospels when the frightened disciples fled from Jesus in the garden of Gethsemane. We assembled in the chapel, and the service went quite normally until we got to the last hymn, which was that great old Easter anthem:

O come, O come, Immanuel,
and ransom captive Israel.

While about 40 men were singing this with great gusto, one of the students began to recite Psalm 22 in a very loud voice over the top of the singing. This is the psalm of a person who feels himself utterly deserted by God and man, echoed by the Lord Jesus during his agony on the cross: "My God, my God, why have you forsaken me?" (Ps 22:1)

The effect of this combination was electric. At the same time as this dramatic duet was continuing, some students came forward and quickly stripped the chapel of all ornamentation. Religious pictures, candles, crucifixes, coverings—anything that could be moved was stripped and removed from our sight. The lights were turned out, creating a somewhat gloomy atmosphere.

As soon as the hymn with the dramatic Bible over-reading was finished, all in the chapel were encouraged to pretend they were the disciples abandoning Jesus in the garden of Gethsemane. We were to get out of the chapel as quickly as possible by whatever means, including diving out the windows! As I was next to one of the windows, and the sill was reasonably low, I climbed up on it prepared to enter into the spirit of the occasion. However, right under my window was one of those plants I described earlier—the ones with long, straight leaves and something approaching iron spikes at the tips. I stood there calculating whether I could leap over this plant, dressed in a cassock, without doing myself some serious harm. I was still in fairly good physical condition in those days, but it was a toss-up. Finally I chickened out and exited quietly by the main door, hands in my pockets.

Now I am not a person who is attracted to religious ritual. I feel a strong affinity with CS Lewis, who, in his autobiography *Surprised by Joy*, admitted that he was ill-suited to most forms of church practice even though he regularly attended chapel services at his college in Oxford in order to 'nail his colours to the mast'. Although the medieval flavour of my theological college was not to my liking, I was aware that many of the students and staff found it attractive and useful, and I would have been willing at that stage of my life to go along with this very high-church flavour if that was all that was involved.

Loaves and sandbars

I said that the college described itself as 'Liberal Catholic'. I must now try to explain what the 'Liberal' part meant. The term 'liberal' is often used in academic circles to mean *broad*; so one often hears it said that a person has had a liberal—that is, a broad—education. It is common in the USA for students to undertake a Liberal Arts degree.

But within the context of a Christian theological institution, the term 'liberal' takes on a particular flavour, a special meaning that parts of the Bible are to be considered suspect, and may not be a true historical record of what actually happened or what was originally written. To give an example, many liberal scholars say that when the Bible records that Jesus fed 5000 people with a few loaves and fishes, no supernatural miracle actually took place. The crowd was so moved by Jesus' teaching about loving one another, it is reasoned, that they all began to share their food together. One cynic has suggested that, within that social context, this may have been a greater miracle than that which Jesus performed!

On another occasion, according to a liberal interpretation, when the disciples saw what they thought and later recorded was Jesus walking on water, he was really walking on a sandbar, and they were mistaken.[2]

Some liberal theologians argue that we live in a rational scientific age in which we can no longer believe in the

....

2. I believe it was Mark Twain who, reacting to the high price tourists were being charged to take a boat ride on the Lake of Galilee, was heard to remark, "It's no wonder Jesus walked!"

miraculous, at least not in the old supernatural sense of the word. If we are, as Christians, to relate to modern people, then the Bible needs to be 'de-mythologized'; that is, the miraculous content needs to be pruned out. If we can strip the Bible of some parts that, they reason, are no longer credible to modern scientific society, then the message of the church will be more easily accepted by the community at large, and the Christian gospel will be taken more seriously.

In fact, the opposite has been shown generally to be the case over the last century or so. In churches and denominations where a liberal approach to the Bible has dominated, average church membership age has tended to increase, and consequently numbers have diminished as the older generation of loyal church members has died off. Generally speaking, liberal theology has been demonstrated to lack the power to attract and hold younger people. In contrast, churches and denominations that hold to what is termed to be a conservative view of the trustworthiness of Scripture have tended to attract the younger generation and grow, or at least hold their own, in an increasingly secular society. It is my personal observation from working full-time as a Christian minister for many years with university students that liberal theology holds little attraction for the younger generation.

The very first lecture note I took down at my new theological institution was on the subject of the Old Testament. The lecturer informed us, "We can no longer believe the Old Testament is the word of God in its entirety". We were told that many of the events of the Old Testament, such as the Exodus from Egypt and the dividing of the Red Sea, probably did not happen. These had their roots in the folklore of Israel and were subsequently added to the text.

The problem that began to disturb me, however, was that

this process did not end with sandbars or loaves and fishes. This liberal approach to the biblical narrative began to take wings so that even central Christian tenets, onto which the historic Christian church has held for about 2000 years, were coming under its scrutiny. There seemed to me to be a sort of academic competitive spirit that had set in, in which your scholastic status was measured by how daring you were willing to be, how far you were willing to press your liberalism. Some students expressed their disbelief in the virgin birth, and I was aware that some liberal scholars even cast doubt upon the physical resurrection of Jesus from the dead— one of the two central foundation stones of Christianity, along with the cross of Jesus. Some of these writers were quoted with approval in my college.

Struggle

I had just come through an 18-month spiritual struggle to arrive, by God's grace, at Christian faith. I found that same faith now being called into question, and even undermined, by the very source that I hoped would strengthen it. The thing that troubled me most was that this process seemed to be quite arbitrary. One student or staff member accepted the virgin birth of Jesus; another rejected it. One believed in miracles; another would deny some miracles but retain others; and another would cast doubt on all of them. Some scholars held to the physical resurrection of Jesus; others said it would not affect their faith if the bones of Jesus were found in Palestine.

This appeared to be rather like a designer religion that you could personally shape to whatever form you found acceptable and comfortable, or like a cafeteria religion in which you could pick and choose the parts that you liked, and reject the rest. As mentioned before, I increasingly perceived a kind of subtle academic competition that developed, in which one's scholarly standing was judged by how daring one was willing to be: "You may deny the loaves and fishes, but *I* deny the virgin birth!"

Had I been more pastorally minded at the time, I might also have been concerned that some of the students were about to be ordained, and would take their doubts into their churches and pulpits. But at the time I was just concerned with my own spiritual survival.

Holy mysteries

Back in the chapel, another problem was beginning to form in my mind. I have always loved those words in the Anglican *Book of Common Prayer* in which the meaning of the death of Christ on the cross is described:

> [He] made there (by his one oblation of himself once offered) a full, perfect, and sufficient sacrifice, oblation, and satisfaction, for the sins of the whole world.

English cannot be made clearer or more precise than that, it seems to me. During my short Christian life I had read enough Roman Catholic literature to understand that denomination's view of the Mass. Catholicism teaches that God, acting through the ordained priest, physically changes the bread and wine into the reality of the body and blood of Christ (a process called transubstantiation), and that the elements are then offered to God as a sacrifice for sins, as a continuation or repetition of the cross of Calvary. I had also come to understand that at the time of the Reformation, this view was universally rejected by the reformers, including the Anglican leaders who were subsequently burned at the stake specifically for this rejection. But in our chapel's Holy Communion services, also now called the Mass, the old interpretation seemed to have made a comeback.

We were encouraged to worship the consecrated bread

and wine, with some students fully spread-eagling themselves facedown in front of it. A phrase had also been inserted into the communion service that began, "We offer these holy mysteries…" Naively, I began to ask about the nature of these "holy mysteries" we were offering, and was told that we were offering ourselves to God as living sacrifices (Rom 12:1). Now, I know some Christians who may be described as "holy mysteries", but I came to the conclusion that a veiled attempt was being made to turn the communion service into a sacrificial offering along Roman Catholic lines.

Morning tea was held each day in the students' common room. Around the common room were newspapers and church periodicals from various parts of Australia and beyond. One particular publication appeared to incur the displeasure of some of the student body, and it contained the news and views of another Anglican Diocese within Australia. As I read it, it seemed harmless enough, so I enquired what it was about that Diocese that was causing their ire. The problem seemed to be that this branch of the Anglican Church was described as 'low church', meaning that services in their churches were rather plain and they did not practise much in the way of ritual. I was told that they were 'evangelical', a term which was foreign to me.

Some of the negativity also seemed to be directed towards their theological college, which as far as I could make out was their main training institution for preparing people for the ministry. Apparently the term 'evangelical' meant they did not adopt the liberal approach to the Scriptures that characterized the methodology of our college. Cautiously, I enquired where this place might be.

Changing course

In short, at the end of Easter I wrote to this evangelical college asking whether it would be willing to accept my transfer for the second term. My application was graciously accepted.

My parents must have been bewildered at what was transpiring. They had found it hard to cope with my giving up the profession of architecture, at least for the present, and must have been even more mystified by this sudden transfer away from home.

Though he was only 56, my father was not a well man. He was a chronic asthmatic, had suffered his first heart attack in his thirties, and had recently survived a major operation for lung cancer. His marriage to my mother was probably just hanging together for the sake of my younger sister, who was still at home. As he felt he was not going to live much longer, at that time he gave each of his three children a generous financial gift in order to circumvent the death duties in place at that time in our state. This was a gracious provision from God, as I had to pay for my own tuition, board and living expenses during my four-year stay at the new college. By the grace of God, these funds, supplemented by money from holiday jobs, lasted me for the whole time. They ran out during the last week of my studies. I sincerely believe this to have been God's remarkable provision.

At the end of the second term in my first college year I travelled home for the holiday break. My father met me at the train station. That night I heard a commotion coming from their bedroom, and my mother urgently calling for me to go and get the doctor who lived next door. My father had suffered a massive heart attack that night and died quickly, a sad and lonely man. I was glad to have spent some time with him that day.

I have made three very excellent decisions in my life. The

first was to believe in Jesus, and to know him in this life and for the life beyond; the second was to ask Marion to be my wife; and the third was in transferring to my new theological college. They put the Bible back in my hands.

three

THE CALL OF GOD IN THE OLD TESTAMENT

Oh, no—here we go again!

I was sitting at the dining room table of my new theological college some time after arriving, and I innocently asked one of my fellow students what he proposed to do after he finished his studies at college. As you can imagine, this was a topic of intense interest for all of us. What should one do? Should one go into full-time Christian service, or perhaps return to previous secular employment—in my case, to the building industry?

"I feel God is calling me to be a missionary in Vanuatu", he replied.

Transferring from one training institution to another solved most of the problems that had troubled me previously. In my new college, the Bible was consistently honoured as the word of the living God, as Jesus himself had so honoured it. Also, we were encouraged in our lectures to study it seriously, not treat it as some form of academic plaything, and to treasure its saving message, or rather to treasure the God who has portrayed himself within its pages. As we had opportunity, we were to convey this message to as many as would pay attention. The chapel services were fairly plain, which suited me, though by today's standards they may have been considered a bit formal.

There was no attempt or desire to attach any adoration or worship to the bread and wine in the Holy Communion. They were reminders of Christ's once-for-all redemptive work upon the cross of Calvary, a work completed in his final shout of triumph, "It is finished!" If we fed upon Christ's body and blood in the Lord's Supper at all, it was to be a spiritual, not literal, feeding. The elements of bread and wine were to be a visual sermon and feast to our eyes and senses, as the reading and exposition of God's word was to be a meal for our ears. By both meals our faith was to be fed and strengthened.

All in all, the move to change training institutions was one of the most strategic and life-changing decisions I have ever made, by God's grace.

However, at least one residual problem continued to hang over me from the past. When I had settled into my new situation, I found I was still surrounded by men and women saying things like, "I feel God is calling me into the ministry"; "I feel God is calling me to work with students"; and "I feel God is calling me to be a missionary in country x". I continued to be somewhat troubled and mystified by this language, because I was not feeling anything of this nature. I began to think that in some way I was missing out on something important, or maybe I was significantly lacking in spirituality. Occasionally I would enquire of someone who was making this kind of I-feel-God-is-calling-me statement, "Tell me, what does it feel like?" to which the answer sometimes came back, "Oh, you will know when it happens!" I did not find this kind of reply to be very helpful, because it never did happen, and it still never has, and as I will try to explain later, I believe it *usually* never will.

Some years after leaving college, and having finally decided to enter into full-time Christian ministry, I found myself being asked to write references for people who 'felt called' into the ministry or to the mission field or to some other form of full-time Christian vocation. Because of the frustration I was experiencing with this issue, I decided to do a study of the word 'call' in the Bible in general, and in the Greek New Testament in particular. The question I set myself was this:

> Does the Bible as a whole, and the New Testament in particular, teach that Christian people must have an inner sense of divine call before they can be considered for ministry ordination, missionary service or a position within some Christian enterprise?

For there is no doubt that this is a big question, particularly for those who regard the Bible as the final arbiter in matters of faith, belief and Christian living—as, according to the gospels, Jesus himself did (for example, in Mark 7:6-13). Nearly every person who applies to be ordained or approaches some missionary agency or seeks a position with some Christian organization will be asked about their sense of call, or will feel obliged to say that a feeling of call and conviction is strongly present.

The following is a summary of my investigation into the biblical use of this term 'call'. The call of God, particularly as it relates to important leaders in the Old Testament who received a definite call (people like Abraham, Moses and Isaiah) could be described like this:

> The word of God comes directly and personally to one of God's people, specifically directing that individual to assume a defined role or task as God's chosen leader, representative or spokesperson.

This definition of the concept of 'call' is deliberately worded to cover a wider group than just the prophets, of whose call Isaiah's is the classic example. It covers other key groups of people as well, such as judges, kings and high priests. The epistle to the Hebrews says, "No [high priest] takes this honour for himself, but only when *called* by God, just as Aaron was" (Heb 5:4). However, it needs to be pointed out that in the later history of Israel, kings and high priests were often appointed by hereditary succession.

'Call' in the Old Testament

The word 'call' is not used a great deal in the sense I have defined it even in the Old Testament, though the *concept* of 'call' as defined occurs frequently. The Lord seems to have employed a dizzying array of methods when calling individuals to assume leadership roles, sometimes much against their will or assessment of their own adequacy for the task.

- With the commissioning of Moses to lead Israel out of bondage in Egypt, God "*called* to him out of the [burning] bush" (Exod 3:4). Moses sees a miraculous sign (the burning bush) and physically hears the voice of God addressing him.
- An angel speaks to Gideon, and Gideon is commissioned by God to lead the army of Israel against the Midianites (Judg 6:12-14), his leadership being confirmed twice by the strange signs of dew falling and then not falling upon a sheepskin (Judg 6:36-40).
- The child Samuel wakes up in the middle of the night hearing the audible voice of God (how I longed to hear that voice!)—"the LORD *called* Samuel" (1 Sam 3:4).
- On other occasions God's choice of a leader is revealed through one of the prophets. For example, when Saul is chosen to be the first king over Israel, this choice is mediated through the prophet Samuel: "the LORD told [Samuel], 'Here is the man of whom I spoke to you! He it is who shall restrain my people'" (1 Sam 9:17).

- Later Samuel is directed to convey God's rejection of the disobedient Saul (1 Sam 15:26) and to anoint the young David as Saul's replacement (1 Sam 16:13).
- Each of the prophets Isaiah and Ezekiel receives his call through the medium of an overwhelming ecstatic vision, which causes Isaiah to blurt out his famous response, "Here am I! Send me" (Isa 6:8).
- On one dramatic occasion the mantle of one prophet, Elijah, as he is taken up to heaven, is passed on physically to his successor Elisha (2 Kgs 2:11-14).
- The farmer Amos, describing his unexpected commission to preach to the recalcitrant northern kingdom of Israel, simply recalls, "the LORD took me from following the flock, and the LORD said to me, 'Go, prophesy to my people Israel'" (Amos 7:15).

However, in many cases in the Old Testament record, we simply are not told how it happened. Even in the foundational call of Abram to be the patriarch of God's chosen people and the first step in God's saving covenantal plan, we are merely told, "The LORD said to Abram" (Gen 12:1). How this happened, or by what methodology God spoke to the patriarch, is not recorded.

This is also true in the case of many of the prophets. The prophecies of Jeremiah and Jonah, for example, simply begin with the words, "Now the word of the LORD came to…" though there is no doubting the reality of the call, as Jeremiah is immediately told, "Before I formed you in the womb I knew you… I appointed you a prophet to the nations" (Jer 1:5). Again, how God spoke is not recorded for us.

In some cases, no information at all is given as to how the person was called to a leadership or prophetic role, as, for example, with Elijah, Daniel and Nahum. In the appointment of the later kings and high priests, heredity alone often determined the person chosen.

There is incredible colour and variety in the Old Testament to describe the ways in which God speaks to people in calling them to be prophets, judges, leaders, high priests and kings—a variety that well exceeds the examples given here.

But one thing that stands out to me is this: when a person is called, you will never read of that person saying, "I *feel* the Lord is calling me to be a prophet" or to take on some other role. Nor do you ever read of a potential leader being asked the question, "Do you *feel* God is calling you to this position?" Noah is not asked how he feels about building an ark, and Abram is not invited to arise and go to the land God has promised *if* he feels this is the will of God for him. In the evidence available through specific examples in the Scriptures, the call of God is external to the person receiving it: an audible voice, a burning bush, a falling mantle, a vision, an angelic visitation. In other cases the evidence is either missing or silent; but where we do have the biblical evidence, it is external to the person being called, and is usually in the form of a command not an invitation.

Now this is quite different from the way in which the word 'call' is being used today. When someone says, "I feel God is calling me", usually they do not mean that they have received some form of externally observable or objective divine visitation. If you inquire as to the nature of this felt call, the person will usually reply that they are experiencing an inward spiritual impression, perhaps with a strong conviction, and that they take this impression to be the guidance of God. However, you will never find this kind of language in the Old Testament. You do not find Isaiah, for instance, saying later that he experienced an inward spiritual impression that he should take up the prophetic role. Instead he says:

In the year that King Uzziah died I *saw* the Lord sitting up on a throne, high and lifted up...

And I *heard* the voice of the Lord saying, "Whom shall I send, and who will go for us?" Then I said, "Here am I! Send me." And he said, "Go, and say to this people..." (Isa 6:1, 8-9)

four

THE CALL OF GOD IN THE NEW TESTAMENT—

JESUS AND THE APOSTLES

As we pass from the pages of the Old Covenant into the New, this model of overt divine visitation continues, at least for a while. The critical question looming on our horizon is this: can we take the examples of the call of God that we find in the Old Testament, and even the specific call of Jesus and the apostles to their ministries, and apply them as normative to the 21st-century church situation? We will examine this question later.

For now, we will observe that the Old Testament pattern of specific, objective divine call continues well into the narrative of the New Testament.

- The priest Zechariah is serving in the temple when "there appeared to him an angel of the Lord" (Luke 1:11). During this external, visual visitation he is told that the birth of his son, to be called John, is in fulfilment of the ancient prophecy that Elijah, or someone very like him, would usher in the Messianic age (Mal 4:5-6; Luke 1:16). When Zechariah expresses his disbelief in the Lord's message, he and his people are given another graphic and measurable sign: he will not be allowed to speak until the baby is born (Luke 1:20).

- Similar external manifestations accompany the birth of Jesus. Mary herself is visited by the same archangel Gabriel. When she is told she is to bear a son, she, like Zechariah, asks the question, "How will this be...?" (Luke 1:34). It is interesting that she is not punished as Zechariah was for asking a very similar question: "How shall I know this?" (Luke 1:18). However, there is a difference. Zechariah questioned the power of God to do such a thing, to give an aged childless couple a baby. Zechariah should have been aware of a number of precedents from God's previous dealings with Israel, from the time of Abraham on. Mary's question, however, is a moral one: "How will this be, since I am a virgin?" (Luke 1:34). Abraham and Sarah's child may have been miraculous, but he was conceived by the normal process. Mary has no access to that process, at least not at this stage.

- Mary's betrothed, Joseph, also receives divine guidance, on this occasion through dreams. In the first dream he is told to go ahead with his plan to marry Mary, and not to proceed with the mooted separation and divorce (Matt 1:19-21). In a subsequent dream, he is commanded to take his new wife and the baby Jesus down to Egypt to escape from Herod's cruelty (Matt 2:13). This act of going down to and returning from Egypt is later seen in itself to have outstanding significance by the Gospel writers, as Matthew records: "This was to fulfil what the Lord had spoken by the prophet, 'Out of Egypt I *called* my son'" (Matt 2:15). God had already called one 'son' out of Egypt: the consistently rebellious Israel, who had been an habitual and abject failure and had ended up as captive slaves in Babylon. Later, God had allowed a pitiful few to return to the rubble-heap that had become Jerusalem. Now God brings another son out of Egypt, one who will be very different to the first. He will be habitually obedient, even to death upon a cross.

- When Jesus begins his adult ministry and comes to be baptized by John the Baptist in the Jordan River, again there is an external manifestation. The Holy Spirit descends upon Jesus in the form of a dove, and a voice is clearly heard out of heaven, "This is my beloved Son, with whom I am well pleased" (Matt 3:16-17). Although Jesus is declared to be the Son of God from his birth—the visible presence of Jehovah walking the earth—there is a special sense in which he stands in the line of the Old Testament prophets. For 30 years, Jesus has lived without blemish before God and man as a child, an adolescent, a carpenter, a son, a Son and an Israelite. Unlike Eve in the garden of Eden and Achan during the battle for Jericho, who were both tested and who both failed as a new chapter of God's plan for the human race opened, Jesus has not failed his Father in any way. He has not deviated at all from full obedience to the will of God during his 30 years of testing and preparation. Summing up these 30 years, the voice from heaven testifies, "with [him] I am well pleased". Jesus is commissioned and further empowered for the three years of ministry ahead with an audible voice and a visible dove.

Let us turn now from the commissioning of Jesus to the calling of the disciples to be his followers, and especially those chosen to be termed apostles. Again, we continue to see a pattern of specific, objective divine call. Jesus does not ask for volunteers to join his close group of disciples, nor does he ask the larger band of disciples which of them may feel some form of inner impression that they are being called to the job.

- Jesus goes along by the Sea of Galilee where there are some fishermen who have spent at least part of one day previously with him (John 1:39). He commands, not invites, them to "Come, follow me". Seeing some other fishermen further on, "immediately he *called* them" (Mark 1:17-20).

- Later in the narrative, Jesus determines to appoint some men from the larger group of followers to be termed apostles. Again, Jesus does not say to the larger group, "Now, we are going to have something called apostles. If any of you feel God is calling you to be an apostle, please see me after the Sermon on the Mount!" After a night of prayer, Mark tells us:

> And he went up on the mountain and called to him those whom he desired, and they came to him. And he appointed twelve (whom he also named apostles) so that they might be with him... (Mark 3:13-14).

There is a clear correlation between the number of apostles chosen and the twelve tribes of Israel: "you who have followed me will also sit on twelve thrones, judging the twelve tribes of Israel", he tells them later (Matt 19:28).

To this inner group of twelve, a small number of other apostles are later added. Again, their appointment is not by some subjective inner impression:

- Matthias is chosen to replace Judas not by some inner 'call', but by nomination and the casting of lots by the rest of the apostolic group (Acts 1:26).

- Paul, the apostle to the Gentiles, has the most graphic visitation imaginable by the risen Lord Jesus on the road to Damascus (Acts 9:1-19).

- And how could Barnabas ever forget the prophetic word that came to the leaders of the church in Antioch? "The Holy Spirit said, 'Set aside for me Barnabas and Saul [Paul] for the work to which I have *called* them'" (Acts 13:2).

A note on the uniqueness of the apostles

The New Testament apostles are no ordinary group, for as Paul says in Ephesians 2:19-20, the church is built upon the foundation of the unique revelations given by God to them and passed on to us through their Spirit-inspired records. Your local minister or missionary is not to be a conduit through which extra divinely inspired revelations can be added to this record, as God did through the prophets and apostles. One does hear from time to time of modern day 'prophets' who actually ask their hearers to paste their 'revelations' into the backs of their Bibles as somehow equal to, or an addition to, Scripture. The closing verses of the book of Revelation should dissuade one from such practices:

> I warn everyone who hears the words of the prophecy of this book: if anyone adds to them, God will add to him the plagues described in this book, and if anyone takes away from the words of the book of this prophecy, God will take away his share in the tree of life and in the holy city, which are described in this book. (Rev 22:18-19)

Strictly speaking, these words apply specifically to the book of Revelation; however, since that book describes divine history up to and including the end of time, there is a legitimate sense in which it may be seen as a final coda to the whole of Scripture.

A critical question

By way of reminder, here is how I summarized in chapter 3 the biblical idea of the call of God:

> *The word of God comes directly and personally to one of God's people, specifically directing that individual to assume a defined role or task as God's chosen leader, representative or spokesperson.*

This summary of the concept of the call of God particularly applies to key figures within the Bible narrative, including the Lord Jesus himself. In this overview we have particularly focused upon two groups within that narrative: the *prophets* in the Old Testament and the *apostles* in the New. The word 'call' is not often used of them, although the concept of 'call' as I have defined it is consistently strong in relation to these two groups. The concept of 'feeling called', however, is consistently absent, and cannot be found in Scripture.

Let us now turn to a detailed study of the pages of the Greek New Testament and ask this critical question: can we take this concept of 'call' as it may apply to the prophets and apostles, and fasten it to the church situation as we experience it today?

five

THE USAGE OF 'CALL' IN THE GREEK NEW TESTAMENT

It is important to look at the prolific and multicoloured use of the word 'call' in the New Testament, and especially in the epistles, as we think through how we use such language today.

In the Greek New Testament, the verb 'to call' (*kalein*) and its various cognates is a surprisingly rich term. It occurs more than 300 times, and is used in several different (but sometimes overlapping) ways.

Seven ways 'call' is used

1. 'Call' used for naming people and places

The most common use of the word is its employment in the naming of people, places and things (it is used 69 times in this manner). When Gabriel visits Mary, she is instructed, "You shall *call* his name Jesus" (Matt 1:21).[1]

Other examples of the word 'call' used for naming people

----

1. There is nothing especially sacred about the name 'Jesus'. It is the Greek form of the common Old Testament name 'Joshua', and its correct pronunciation was probably very different from the way we pronounce 'Jesus'. As Joshua led God's people into the promised land of Canaan, so 'our Joshua' has opened the way into the new promised land of heaven.

and places include Simon the magician being described by the people of Samaria as "the power of God that is *called* Great" (Acts 8:10), and the apostle Paul being "*called*... Hermes" (Acts 14:12).[2]

2. 'Call' used as a synonym for 'known as'

In addition, the word 'call' is sometimes used as a kind of synonym for one thing being known for another quality it may possess. So 17 times we find statements like, "My house shall be *called* a house of prayer for all the nations" (Mark 11:17). That is, God desires that his house (the temple in Jerusalem) should be widely known as a place where people can go to pray to God in a spiritually conducive environment without undue obstruction or distraction.

In a similar vein, the prodigal son confesses to his father, "I am no longer worthy to be *called* your son" (Luke 15:19); and Paul later reflects that he is "unworthy to be *called* an apostle" (1 Cor 15:9).

3. 'Call' used as an invitation or command to come

The word is also used 33 times for the extension of an invitation. For example, we are told that "Jesus also was invited [*called*] to the wedding [in Cana] with his disciples" (John 2:2). In another passage Jesus said, "But when you give a feast, invite [*call*] the poor, the crippled, the lame, the blind..." (Luke 14:13).

In many cases the invitation is more of a command to come

....

2. One of Jesus' teachings about which large sections of the Christian church seem to have collective amnesia is "*call* no man your father on earth, for you have one Father, who is in heaven" (Matt 23:9). Jesus gave the church specific teaching on the subject of leaders not taking fancy titles for themselves, or wearing distinctive clothing, which would be seen to place leaders as distinct from or superior in some way to their congregations. In particular, Jesus singled out the term 'Father' as one title church leaders should not use.

to someone or appear before them: "Then Herod summoned [*called*] the wise men secretly and ascertained from them what time the star had appeared" (Matt 2:7); also, when Jesus' mother and brothers arrived to speak with him, "standing outside they sent to him and *called* him" (Mark 3:31).

Very significantly, the word 'call' is also used in this way with respect to the invitation of the gospel. The gospel is a 'call' or invitation that goes out to many but to which only a certain number respond. Thus, the sower goes out to sow and scatters his seed far and wide. It falls in all sorts of places and, depending on the type of soil in which it lands, the seed responds accordingly. Many seeds are scattered but only a small proportion germinate and come to full fruition. This story is probably the most significant of all the parables told by Jesus, since it is all about the God-given ability to receive and understand the word of God. Jesus himself testified, "Do you not understand this parable? How then will you understand all the parables?" (Mark 4:13).

This aspect of the usage of 'call' is summed up in Jesus' simple statement, "Many are *called*, but few are chosen" (Matt 22:14). It is the job of those who carry the message of salvation to scatter the seed wherever and whenever we have the opportunity, or, if we cannot find ready opportunity, to sensitively create opportunity. And is that not all of us to some degree (see, for example, Philippians 2:14-16)? It is solely God's work to take that preached word and create spiritual life. The term 'call' is being used here, and another 18 times, for the general preaching and propagation of the gospel message.

Of his own ministry, Jesus testified, "I came not to *call* the righteous, but sinners" (Matt 9:13). Several times Jesus pictured the offer of the gospel as that of a great dinner feast in which the master commands his servants, "Go therefore to the main

roads and invite [*call*] to the wedding feast as many as you find"
(Matt 22:9).

4. 'Call' used of Jesus coming 'out of Egypt'

As mentioned in the previous chapter, on one occasion 'call'
is used of the child Jesus, as Joseph and Mary bring him back
from the sojourn in Egypt to their own land. Matthew sees
extraordinary significance in the fulfilment of the prophecy,
"Out of Egypt I *called* my son" (Matt 2:15). It is instructive to
look at the original prophecy, found in Hosea 11:1-2, for in the
context it does not seem to be about Jesus directly at all. God
laments,

> When Israel was a child, I loved him,
>   and out of Egypt I called my son.
> The more they were called,
>   the more they went away;
> they kept sacrificing to the Baals
>   and burning offerings to idols. (Hos 11:1-2)

We might well protest, "What is going on here?" Matthew has
taken a verse from its Old Testament context, which refers to
the idolatrous and rebellious nation of Israel at that time, and
applied it directly to the infant Jesus Christ, joining the two
together with the statement, "This was to fulfil what the Lord
had spoken by the prophet". Is it right of the Gospel author to
use the Old Testament Scriptures in this manner?

There are at least two ways in which the New Testament
writers use the prophetic writings from the Old Testament.
These two methods could be termed 'predictive' and 'repetitive'.
'Predictive' prophecy can be summarized as "Look, it is
coming true". In other words, there is a prediction in the Old
Testament which literally comes true in the New. The most
obvious example of this is the prediction that the longed-for

Messiah would be born in the city or town from which King David himself originated, Bethlehem (Mic 5:2). The edict of the Roman Emperor thousands of kilometres away is used by a sovereign God to bring this to literal fulfilment. The suffering servant passages of Isaiah 53 are also essentially predictive.

But some other Old Testament passages are used by the writers of the New Testament in a different manner altogether. These 'repetitive' prophecies may be characterized not as "Look, it's coming true" but rather as "Here we go again!" To express this differently, God has performed some act in the times before Christ, and now he is repeating the dose. God once brought a son (the nation of Israel) out of Egypt, and now he does it again.

The first son, Israel, failed miserably to fulfil God's plans for them at the climax of their Exodus from Egypt. Commanded to enter the Promised Land, they rebelled at Kadesh, talking even of returning to Egypt! The second son, also now coming out of Egypt, will succeed, dramatically highlighted by Jesus' conversation with Moses and Elijah on the mountain of transfiguration: they "spoke of his departure which he was about to accomplish at Jerusalem" (Luke 9:31).

Here is not the place to unwrap this idea of predictive and repetitive prophecy more fully, except to say that from my observation, more cases are probably in the latter category than in the former. Some popular Christian writers tend to lump all prophecy together without regard to the context, and to present their findings as some form of mathematical proof of the rightness of Christianity. Since 'x' prophecies have amazingly come true, they argue, the odds in favour of the Bible being true are several million to one. To treat all prophetic references simply as predictive prophecy appears to be a shallow approach, not taking into account the original Old Testament contexts.

5. 'Call' used of the high priest's appointment

'Call' is also used once for the appointment of a person to be the high priest: "No-one takes this honour for himself, but only when *called* by God, just as Aaron was" (Heb 5:4).

6. 'Call' used as a description of our faith response

Now we must look at the manner in which faith and salvation happen. The word 'call' is used 11 times as a synonym for the response that we term Christian 'belief' or 'faith'. So Peter, preaching on the day of Pentecost and quoting the prophet Joel, expounds the consequence of gospel proclamation: "Everyone who *calls* upon the name of the Lord shall be saved" (Acts 2:21). He testifies that we are to *call* upon the name of God by placing our faith, trust and hope in his Son, crucified and risen. We are not to trust in the things we have done for God, but in the great work he has done for us in sending Jesus to be our true 'Joshua'.

Soon after this, Peter again urges the listening crowd to "save yourselves from this crooked generation" (Acts 2:40), giving as his reason "for there is no other name under heaven given among men by which we must be saved" (Acts 4:12). His listeners are to save themselves by calling upon the name of the Lord, placing their faith and trust in the crucified and risen one.

Likewise, when Paul is converted, Ananias instructs him to place his faith in Jesus in this manner: "Rise and be baptized and wash away your sins, *calling* on his name" (Acts 22:16). Calling upon the name of the Lord Jesus is synonymous with genuine, born-again Christian faith. Paul writes: "To the church of God that is in Corinth… together with all those who in every place *call* upon the name of our Lord Jesus Christ" (1 Cor 1:2).

Peter also expresses such faith in this manner: "if you *call* on him as Father who judges impartially according to each one's deeds, conduct yourselves…" (1 Pet 1:17).

7. 'Call' used as a description of new birth and election

If the New Testament looks at the process of becoming a true believer 11 times from the point of view of our faith, far more often it goes 'through the looking glass', describing salvation as perceived from God's side.

Paul often speaks in this way: "God, who saved us and *called* us to a holy *calling…*" (2 Tim 1:8-9). In these 39 uses, the word is being employed as we might use the technical expression 'regeneration', otherwise described as 'new birth' or even 'birth from above' (John 3:1-15). Regeneration is entirely something God does to and for us, not something we do for ourselves or for God. We, who are in a spiritually comatose state due to our sin and rebellion; who are insensitive to any word from God and impervious to any merely human spiritual stimulation; who are in chains and bondage to our own selfishness and self-centredness; he has awakened and set free by his Spirit. This act we call regeneration, and unless you have experienced it, Jesus says, you will never understand or experience heaven (John 3:3).

The New Testament exhorts us 11 times to *call* upon the name of the Lord by faith, as described above. More than three times as often it testifies that the initiative rests with God to *call* us by new birth into his kingdom, simply because he chooses to do so by his mercy. In the process by which you and I come to salvation, the emphasis is strongly upon the sovereignty of God.

You often hear believers talking about 'free will', by which they seem to imply that God has given people the ability to freely accept or reject Jesus Christ.

Now it is true that in daily life we do appear to have a limited range of 'free will' experiences. Every day we make choices about what to eat and what clothes to wear. But even these choices may be limited by whether we have food and clothing, and, if we do, by the range of choices we can afford.

If you have only one shirt, you can choose whether to wear it or not—but that is the limit of your choice. We can also make more significant choices such as whom to marry or which car to buy. But again, these choices are limited: the first by the range of other people willing to marry you, and the latter by available funds. However, most people would say we seem to experience a range of 'free will' choices.

Consequently, many people speak of their 'free will' ability to choose God or to reject him. This, I believe, is both dangerous and in error. For a start, God only ever gives us one choice— that is, to repent, believe and receive his Son as Lord and Saviour. The call to salvation is not an open-ended, take-it-or-leave-it invitation, but a command. "[God] commands all people everywhere to repent" (Acts 17:30), Paul tells the philosophical idol-bound Athenians.

Secondly, we are incapable of making this choice simply 'off our own bat', because our wills in this matter are in bondage to insidious sin. I prefer to speak of '*freed* will' rather than 'free will'. When our stubborn, sin-bound wills are set free by the word of God acting together with the regenerating work of the Spirit, then and only then will a person come to faith in Jesus Christ. "For the law of the Spirit of life has set you free in Christ Jesus from the law of sin and death", says Paul (Rom 8:2).

I once saw on television an experiment carried out in space. An astronaut dressed only in singlet and shorts was floating at rest in the space vehicle, with his extended arm about a metre from the wall. He was told to move himself to the wall. Being free from gravity, he began to twist, tumble, turn and freely perform all sorts of gymnastic manoeuvres. But whenever he could stop himself and hold out his arm, he was still *exactly* the same distance from the wall. We all have a physical centre of gravity, the commentator explained, and all the astronaut could do was to spin around it—he could not move it. He was, in fact, in a terrible form of bondage to his own centre of gravity, and needed help from someone else to remove him from the situation. Unless this happened he could die from starvation.

The Bible says the same about our condition before God. We appear to be free to make all kinds of decisions every day of the week—what food to eat, what clothes to put on—and bigger decisions like whom to marry and which house or car to buy. But in relation to God, we are, of ourselves, in spiritual bondage to sin and our own spiritual centre of gravity; to our own selfishness and self-centredness. Unless another delivers us from this dangerous situation we will die, and that deliverance is exactly what God has provided so wonderfully for us in Christ. As Jesus himself testified, "everyone who practices sin is a slave to sin" (John 8:34) and, in another place, "So if the Son sets you free, you will be free indeed" (John 8:36).

Paul stresses God's primary initiative in the process of salvation as being akin to his initial work of creation, speaking of "God… who gives life to the dead and *calls* into existence the things that do not exist" (Rom 4:17), and later, "that God's purpose of election might continue, not because of works but because of him who *calls*" (Rom 9:11). The writer of the epistle to the Hebrews likewise addresses believers as those "who share in a heavenly *calling*" (Heb 3:1).

This aspect of the usage of 'call' (as a description of our response to the gospel) is also often related to Christian sanctification or holiness. If we have heard and heeded the call of God to become disciples of his son Jesus as it has come to us by the proclamation of the good news through whatever means; if we have been spiritually awakened and called into his kingdom by the divine work of regeneration (new birth or birth from above); and if we have consequently begun by faith and repentance to call upon the name of the Lord; then our lives should, or rather must, be changed by this experience, and always for the better. As Paul puts it, "For God has not *called* us for impurity, but in holiness" (1 Thess 4:7).

Addressing the freedom-hungry Galatian Christians, Paul exhorts them:

> For you were *called* to freedom, brothers. Only do not use your freedom as an opportunity for the flesh, but through love serve one another. (Gal 5:13)

Similarly, he encourages the Ephesian church to "walk in a manner worthy of the *calling* to which you have been *called*" (Eph 4:1).

We hear this gong being struck 20 times in the New Testament—if our response to the call to be Christ's followers is genuine and not fraudulent, this will be shown by a changed lifestyle. In fact, without holiness no-one will ever see the Lord, we are warned consistently. The good tree is known by its fruit; faith without works is dead.

Special note 1: calling and the church

When Paul was in Ephesus, a riot broke out as a result of the growth of Christianity in the city (Acts 19). The sales of trinkets and tourist items at the pagan temple of Artemis were apparently dropping off. The craftsmen who made these items instigated a two-hour riot in the theatre, and the word used for this unruly gathering is usually translated into English as 'assembly' in Acts 19:32 and again in verse 41. The word in Greek is actually *ekklesia*, which has our Greek word *kalein* ('to call') buried within it. So *ek* ('out') plus *kalein* ('called') might literally be taken in this context as "a group of people who have been called out".[3]

....

3. R Earle, *Word Meanings in the New Testament*, one-volume edn, Beacon Hill Press, Kansas City, Kindle edn, 2011.

This is the word that is also used for 'church' 115 times throughout the New Testament. However, there is general agreement among biblical scholars that although the word may have had its origins in the idea of 'called out ones', by the time of the New Testament it simply meant a 'congregation' or 'assembly'.[4]

It is clear from the pages of the New Testament that it was part of Jesus' primary plan to gather together an assembly of God's people, both now on earth and finally in heaven (Rev 7:9). "You are Peter", Jesus says to the apostle, "and on this rock I will build my *ekklesia*, and the gates of hell shall not prevail against it" (Matt 16:18).

This is demonstrated clearly in the strategic plan of the apostle Paul. Wherever Paul travelled on his missionary journeys, he planted churches—that is, groups of local believers who were encouraged to continue to gather together. Paul did not simply tell them the gospel and then depart leaving them to think about what he had said, as if it was merely the latest philosophical topic, the flavour of the month for discussion. He deliberately brought them together into church gatherings for regular teaching and fellowship.

It is fashionable in our freewheeling culture for people to say, "I believe in Jesus, but not in the church", and try to live out their lives without belonging to a local assembly. The Lord Jesus and the apostles knew nothing of such a pattern of behaviour. In fact, such an attitude flies in the face of the expressed wishes and design of our Lord, and can have eternal and fatal consequences.

....

4. See, for example, G Kittle and G Friedrich (eds), *Theological Dictionary of the New Testament*, abridged edn, comp. GW Bromiley, Eerdmans, Grand Rapids, 1985, p. 401.

Special note 2: 'call' in the Pastoral Epistles

Particular attention must be drawn to three little books in the New Testament collectively and commonly given the title "the Pastoral Epistles". These consist of 1 and 2 Timothy and Titus. Timothy and Titus were two church leaders and compatriots of the apostle Paul, and in these epistles he gives them instructions as to the development of leadership within the infant church. Several times Paul spells out the qualifications that should be looked for in Christian leadership.

The importance of these three little books for the church today, or in any era, cannot be overstated. In particular, Paul discusses the qualification for a person to be *presbuteros*, usually translated in English as 'elder'. Today we usually call such a person a 'pastor' or 'minister', although in the New Testament, a church may have a group of *presbuteroi*. In a subsequent chapter I will look in more detail at these qualifications, but one requirement you will never find in the Pastoral Epistles, or anywhere else within the New Testament for that matter, is this: you will never find Paul or any other writer saying, "Do make sure that the candidate for leadership has a strong sense or feeling of being *called* to the position". Never.

To what are we called?

In summary, based on these 300-plus uses of the word 'call' as they relate to the church period following the ministries of Jesus and the apostles, you and I are called by God in two ways:

- **First, we are called to be Christians—to be disciples of Jesus.**
- **Second, we are called to be holy—to grow in Christlikeness.**

If we accept these two statements, then I believe answers to all the other questions about guidance and vocation will be much more straightforward. But let me say one more time that the concept of 'feeling called' to some particular Christian service finds no support within Scripture.

Just semantics?

You may think that this is merely a haggling over terminology. What does it matter what words we use, you may ask, provided it gets the job done? But I want to suggest that there are two nasty practical and pastoral problems that flow from a consistently unbiblical use of the term 'call', especially the commonly heard 'feeling called'.

The first is that such usage may be used as an excuse for Christian laziness or even fear. I believe many Christians, in misguided piety, think to themselves, "I would not dare to serve the Lord until I receive a definite and personal call from him to do so. I do not 'feel called' to be a church minister, so it would be wrong of me even to consider it." They may think, "I do not feel a specific 'call' to be a missionary, so there is no point in my applying. In fact, it would be wrong of me to do so." Similarly, "I am willing to use and develop my gifts within the fellowship of God's church, once the Lord reveals to me the specific gifts I am to exercise. Until then it is best if I leave it up to others." Or: "I have not received the 'call' to be an evangelist, as our pastor clearly has, and I will support him to the hilt, but it would be detrimental to the kingdom for me even to try to share my faith". People may not say such things in public, of course—it might sound rather unspiritual. This thinking may even be largely subconscious. But this concept of 'feeling called', I believe, can often be used as a cop-out from Christian responsibility.

The second pastoral area concerns Christian 'failure'. According to one group in Australia that helps burned-out ministers, something like 50 percent of all ordained pastors or ministers end up giving up that specific role and doing something else, many returning to secular employment. But how can a person give up the personal call of God? Jeremiah tried it once:

> If I say, "I will not mention him,
>   or speak any more in his name",
> there is in my heart as it were a burning fire
>   shut up in my bones,
> and I am weary with holding it in,
>   and I cannot. (Jer 20:9)

I would be willing to claim that nearly every person who has been ordained in Australia or who has applied for missionary service has expressed, or been asked to profess, a distinct sense of divine and personal call to the role. But to my mind, this places an unfair and unbiblical guilt trip upon the person. If Christian workers should fail in their ministry or have to give up, are they forsaking the call of God? Are they being an 'un-Jeremiah'? People give up all kinds of ministries for all kinds of good reasons: burnout, culture shock, discovered unsuitability not apparent previously, attacks by other believers, sickness, disillusionment, or lack of support and care.

I met a missionary couple with a terrible story some time ago. The husband was the principal of a Bible college in another culture. His wife was asked to give a talk at a women's rally. Her talk was to be translated into the local language by an indigenous Christian woman. As the principal's wife spoke, unknown to her, the translator was using the occasion to settle private scores with some women in the congregation, using their names. Of course, everyone thought these rebukes were coming from the speaker! As outsiders, the missionary couple could never prove their innocence, and eventually had to leave their 'calling' and come home in total despair. Is it possible for a believer to do that to another fellow Christian? Of course it is. It should not happen, but it does. Now to say to this couple, "You have failed God by giving up your calling" would be cruel.

When the going gets tough

One missionary leader has responded to me, "But if you take away the need for a definite call, what motivation will there be for a person to continue when the going gets tough?" This is a fair question, but we must, as evangelicals, seek the answer from Scripture and not from some artificially contrived theology that, I have argued, has no basis within its pages. There is an answer, but we must look elsewhere for it. Why should any person go into the ministry, or be a missionary, or do anything in the name of our Lord?

I will attempt to provide an answer in a subsequent chapter, but first I need to deal with a serious and often-heard objection to what I have argued above: "But what about someone like Hudson Taylor?"

six

DID GOD CALL HUDSON TAYLOR?

The play was well in progress when the strange figure suddenly jumped on the stage and called on the proceedings to stop. The fact that he was dressed in Chinese clothes and had a traditional black pigtail hanging down his back was not in itself remarkable, since the play was taking place in rice fields not far from the Chinese city of Nanxun. What surprised the thousands gathering around was that, on closer scrutiny, the man appeared to be European.

The strange figure looked over the heads of the audience to the stalls that surrounded the stage and offered gambling and seductively dressed prostitutes.

"Pity your own souls. Don't be bait to lure others to endless damnation!" he admonished the actors participating in the immoral play. Then turning to the audience he called out, "What you see all around you is wrong. Isn't what I am saying true?"

But this time the organizers were ready for him. He and his companion had interrupted the proceedings on the two previous evenings, even preaching from a ladder erected at the back of the audience. "Would you like your own daughters to be in the state of these women?" they had called out. "Then why buy other men's daughters for immoral purposes?" they asked, to some approval from the crowd.

Hudson Taylor and his Scottish companion were firmly, without violence, evicted from the play and its surrounds. That night and in the following days they continued to distribute Chinese tracts and New Testaments in the town, and to preach wherever they could find opportunity, even to the Buddhist monks at the local shrines.

China Inland Mission

The year was 1855, and the young Hudson Taylor had travelled from England to China to bring the gospel of salvation to this largely neglected country. In the early days of his ministry Taylor often worked alone, but by the time of his death in 1905 aged 73, over 800 missionaries evangelized under the banner of the China Inland Mission that he had founded.

Taylor is probably the best known and most admired missionary leader of the last century and a half. The mission he founded continues today as the Overseas Missionary Fellowship (OMF).

I have chosen Hudson Taylor as representative of a wider group of missionaries, both in former times and today, who have described their decision to go to the mission field as a response to the call of God. In his OMF-published biography, *J Hudson Taylor: A Man in Christ*, Roger Steer records Taylor as saying, "God has *called* me to spend my life in missionary service in China", and, on an earlier occasion, "The conviction has never left me that I was *called* to China" (emphasis mine).[1]

I am quoting Hudson Taylor only as a typical example. I could have quoted William Carey, who in former days went to

....

1. R Steer, *J Hudson Taylor: A Man in Christ*, OMF, Singapore, 1990, pp. 16 and 8.

Bengal; or Amy Carmichael, who went to India; or John Paton, who went to the New Hebrides.

Am I asserting that Hudson Taylor and Christian leaders like him were mistaken in their firmly held and often stated belief that God had personally and clearly called them to their individual ministries? It would seem to be highly arrogant of me or anybody else to question the reality of their call, especially as I am at present writing from the security of a comfortable Western setting and have never experienced anything like the hardship endured by people like Hudson Taylor. Eleven times he made the hazardous journey by sailing ship from England to China, several times facing possible shipwreck. He buried his wife and four of his children in China, all of whom died from local diseases which they probably would not have caught at home in England. Eventually he sent his second wife and remaining children back to the safety of Britain, and carried on!

However, in the long run, as evangelical Christians our doctrines and beliefs must have their foundations in the unchangeable teachings of Scripture and not in variable Christian experience, regardless of how noble or inspirational that experience may have been. So let me come clean at this point and acknowledge that, yes, I am questioning the language of 'feeling called' that was then, and still is today, so frequently employed.

Early days

In trying to understand why Hudson Taylor went to China, we need to examine his upbringing. He was born in 1832 into a godly Christian family who lived in the town of Barnsley in Yorkshire, England. Hudson's father, described as a somewhat reserved, austere figure, ran a chemist shop in the town and was also a Methodist lay preacher, probably a second-generation product of the Wesleyan revival. Steer records the Taylors praying, even before their first child was conceived, "Dear God, if you should give us a son, grant that he may work for you in China".[2] At birth he was given his mother's maiden name, Hudson.

Hudson's father had a particular spiritual interest in the people of the most populous country on earth, China. He was concerned that at the opening of the 19th century not a single Protestant missionary was working in that great country. The father would often question his children:

"What empire is over 100 times the size of England and occupies one-tenth of that area of the earth's surface where people can live?"

"China."

"Correct. If all the Chinese people were ordered to stand in single file, with a yard between each of them, how many times would they circle the globe at the equator?"

"Seven." (Today, more than 20 times!)

"And who invented gunpowder, the compass, paper, and discovered the art of printing?"

"The Chinese."

"Correct."

Hudson, however, in his teenage years, struggled to understand the grace of salvation—not helped by the pressure of his peers. This struggle is winsomely described by JC Pollock in *Hudson Taylor and Maria*:

> [Hudson] believed Christianity to be a dreary struggle to pay off bad deeds by good. He had long abandoned this struggle. He owed too much. He had gone into spiritual bankruptcy, paying a small dividend to his Divine Creditor in the shape of chapel attendance and prayers rattled off at

2. Steer, p. 1.

night but with no hope of discharge; like most bankrupts he had sought to have a good time.[3]

Coming of the light

Shortly after turning 17, and merely to fill in an idle hour, Hudson read a small gospel tract "in an utterly unconcerned state of mind… and with a distinct intention to put away the tract as soon as it should seem prosy".[4] The tract seems to have been a story of the conversion of a coalminer based around the verse from 1 Peter 2:24: "[Christ] himself bore our sins in his body on the tree, that we might die to sin and live to righteousness".

Hudson described this experience in his own words: "And with this dawned the joyful conviction, as light was flashed into my soul by the Holy Spirit, that there was nothing in the world to be done but to fall down on one's knees, and accepting this Saviour and his salvation, to praise him for evermore".[5] The prayers of his family, and especially of his mother and beloved sister, had been answered. From that time on, Hudson Taylor began to commit himself to the daunting work of taking this saving gospel to the millions who lived in China.

Was Hudson Taylor called?

We know a great deal about Hudson's decision to follow this goal because of the thousands of letters he wrote during his lifetime, and his own book, *A Retrospect*. Steer records Hudson's own words, which I quoted only in part earlier. The full quote is this:

....
3. JC Pollock, *Hudson Taylor and Maria: Pioneers in China*, McGraw-Hill, New York, 1962, p. 17.
4. J Hudson Taylor, *A Retrospect*, 3rd edn, China Inland Mission, Toronto, Kindle edn, n.d.
5. ibid.

I felt that I was entering into a covenant with the Almighty. I felt as though I wished to withdraw my promise but could not. Something seemed to say: "Your prayer is answered". And from that time the conviction has never left me that I was called to China.[6]

It is important to notice the language Hudson uses in his own description of his 'call'. You will observe that he uses expressions like, "I *felt* that I was entering"; "I *felt* as though"; "Something *seemed* to say"; and "the *conviction* has never left me".

Now, I do not wish in any way to denigrate the magnificent work done by the China Inland Mission and the other 40 or so mission groups that became active in that country during this period. We can only stand in awe and with great thankfulness to God for the seed-planting work they did under situations of great hardship and at great personal cost. When all the Western missionaries were forced to leave China after Mao's communists came to power in the 1950s, it was estimated that there may have been half a million believers in China.

During the period of the 'Bamboo Curtain', many felt that the Christian church in China may have withered under continual political pressure and persecution.[7] On the contrary, it is estimated that there are between 20 and 60 million believers living in China today. Just this week I have received two invitations from Chinese churches in my own city that have had to expand their premises to cater for the numbers attending. In another city I have heard of dozens of active

....

6. Steer, p. 8.
7. 'Bamboo Curtain' refers to the period 1949-1976, during which mainland China was ruled by Mao Zedong's Communist Party. Christian missionaries were evicted, church attendance was forbidden, and church buildings were adapted for secular uses. Believers were forced to meet secretly in what became known as the 'Underground Church'. Since Mao's death in 1976 the situation for Christians in China has improved in fits and starts.

Chinese congregations. The growth of the gospel among the Chinese people has been one of the great miracles of the last two centuries, which can only cause us to give great praise to our God for his grace.

God used an ordinary man to do extraordinary things. Hudson Taylor agreed with the following unflattering description of himself by a Canadian journalist of the time:

> Hudson Taylor is rather disappointing… A stranger would never notice him in the street… Nor is his voice in the least degree majestic… He displays little oratorical power… He elicits little applause… launches no thunderbolts… Even our Goforth used to plead more eloquently for China's millions, and apparently with more effect.[8]

The language of pietism

However, returning to the point I made in the previous chapter: the sort of language with which Hudson Taylor expressed his decision to go to China cannot be found in the Bible, either in the Old Testament or the New. I do not doubt in any way the reality of Taylor's desire to go to the Chinese people—a desire and commitment that never deserted him throughout his lengthy ministry. However, I would propose that when he spoke of God 'calling' him to leave his home and go to China, he was using the pietistic language that was prevalent in evangelical Christian circles in his day—a language that has persisted to the present. As he attended church and missionary meetings during his formative years, Hudson would have heard this type of expression being used as normative Christian language, just as it continues to be normative in many circles today. It was quite natural and acceptable for him to express his desires in this way.

....

8. Steer, p. 310.

What motivated Hudson Taylor?

If it was (and is) unbiblical to use the terminology of 'feeling called', then what other alternative is there? How else could we describe the motivation that led people like Hudson Taylor to leave the security of familiar surroundings to take the saving gospel of Jesus, crucified and risen, into unfamiliar and often dangerous places? We should also ask a second, more up-to-date question: what should be motivating people today to serve Christ in the gospel, if not by the medium of a felt call?

I will distil six stages through which I believe Hudson Taylor progressed, which resulted in his decision to go to China; for in the long run it was *his decision*.

1. Environment

The first thing to notice is the *environment*. Hudson Taylor grew up in a missionary-minded Christian family. From his earliest years it was impressed upon him that, in gospel terms, so many people in China had so little. England was a relatively small country with a church on almost every corner. China, however, it is said, had not one single Protestant missionary by 1800. (There was a small Catholic work left over from previous times.)

In my experience, very, very few believers today have a 'Damascus road' instantaneous experience that leads them into serious Christian endeavour. Even if a person does not have the benefit of a Christian family upbringing, for most Christians who enter into missionary work there will be a fairly significant period of nurturing, Bible learning and ministry experience, usually within the fellowship of the local church. A time of training in a Bible or theological college will usually follow.

2. Conversion

Hudson Taylor became a genuine Christian after a personal *conversion* to faith and trust in Jesus, and his heart and mind were gripped by the gospel, especially by the atoning work of Christ on the cross.

If I was being asked to examine a person for gospel work today, the first thing I would ask would not be whether there was a felt call, but how the person has come to believe and trust in Jesus. What events have led the person to this point? Is the person's heart gripped by the gospel? As Paul described it, "For the love of Christ controls us" (2 Cor 5:14), and "Woe to me if I do not preach the gospel!" (1 Cor 9:16). Jeremiah described his reluctant ministry of the word in this way: "I am weary with holding it in, and I cannot" (Jer 20:9).

3. Gospel consequences

A person's heart and mind must also be gripped by the *consequences* of the gospel, as Taylor's were. Not only are people saved through the knowledge of the gospel, but men and women who lack this message are described as eternally lost. Ignorance is no excuse, Paul argues in Romans 1-3, when one is confronted with the valid general revelations of creation and conscience. Ephesians 2:1-3 is very revealing in this context. Paul is describing the condition of the people of Ephesus when they were in ignorance of Jesus and his work, and before he, Paul, came and brought to them the gospel. He says they were "dead in the trespasses and sins" (v. 1), and more seriously "were by nature children of wrath, like the rest of mankind" (v. 3).

This understanding of the biblical gospel led Taylor to realize its inevitable conclusion—that without faith in

Christ crucified and risen the Chinese people were on their way to hell, and that their ignorance of God's ways would not excuse them on the last day.

4. Compassion

Mere knowledge of the gospel and its serious consequences is in itself not enough (even if the Bible could be known thoroughly forwards and backwards, with every theological nuance covered). It must be coupled with a deep heartfelt *compassion* for people. When you walk down a thronged street, or watch the crowds at the beach, or are sitting in the grandstand of a sporting complex, is your heart moved with compassion as Jesus' heart was? We are told that he looked on the crowds and "had compassion for them, because they were… like sheep without a shepherd" (Matt 9:36). As Hudson Taylor considered China, he did not see one shepherd looking for one sheep lost on the hills; he saw in his mind 300 million lost sheep, and no shepherd!

5. Action

Even compassion is not enough. Who has not been moved by the scenes of starvation, war and disease with which we are presented almost daily on our television screens? It is very easy to feel the pangs of conscience yet flick over to another channel and in the long run do little or nothing. Taylor's compassion led him to *take action and go*. Over and over we may cry out to God, "Why doesn't someone do something!" but eventually, if we have truly compassionate hearts, we may well begin to ask, "Why not me?"

6. Suitability

Lastly, there should be what I may call *suitability*. The fact that you or I may express a desire to go somewhere for Christ, or undertake some enterprise for the gospel, is usually not sufficient in itself. Taylor first had to be examined and approved by the mission society that sent him out, and usually that will also be the case today. I will say more about this in a subsequent chapter.

One has to be careful, however, with suitability. Selection committees are made up of fallible human beings, and I am sure candidates have been refused who should have been accepted, and vice versa.

These six stages led Hudson Taylor to China, and I believe they should be the motivating forces for those considering a life totally devoted to gospel work: environment, conversion, gospel consequences, compassion, action and suitability. Whether or not a person has a felt call appears to be biblically irrelevant.

Again, some will say this is a mere haggling over terminology, but I wish to repeat something I said in the previous chapter. If we continue to hang onto this unbiblical 'call' language, it will pay us unintended but unfortunate dividends in two areas: some will, through laziness or fear, say "I do not have the 'call', so I need not do anything"; others who do actively respond and for some reason later fail may be left with the guilty impression that they have thrown in the towel and forsaken the call of God. In fact, what they may be doing is simply transferring from one type of ministry to another.

Perhaps we should allow Hudson Taylor to have the last word. He wrote this to those who applied for service with the China Inland Mission:

> If you want hard work and little appreciation; if you value
> God's approval more than you fear man's disapprobation; if
> you are prepared to take joyfully the spoiling of your goods,

and seal your testimony, if need be, with your blood... you may count on a harvest of souls now and a crown of glory hereafter "that fadeth not away", and on the Master's "Well done".[9]

9. Dr and Mrs Howard Taylor, *Hudson Taylor and the China Inland Mission: The growth of a work of God*, Morgan and Scott for China Inland Mission, London, 1919, p. 269.

seven

"THE LORD HAS TOLD ME"

"The Lord is telling me that you are going to have three more children—all at once!"

My wife and I had always wanted to have four children, but after some eight years of marriage the Lord had given us just one child, a son. We had attended various infertility clinics, and although they could not find any physiological problems, eventually they had to tell us that we had run through the full range of tests then on offer. They could do no more for us. Also, by this stage I was considered too old under state law to be eligible to adopt a child, and the fact that we already had a natural child was another strike against us. We began to look into adopting a child from overseas.

At the time, in the church we attended we had a friend who was very godly and prayerful, though occasionally given to making statements beginning with the words, "The Lord has told me…" I believe he saw this as a form of prophetic gifting. We had been confiding in him our desire for more children, and had asked him to pray for us. One day when we were meeting together he came out with this dramatic statement: "The Lord is telling me that you are going to have three more children—all at once!"

Much as we admire the person who made this encouraging

prediction, in fact it has not come true. By the miraculous grace of God we were later able to adopt a beautiful baby girl at two weeks of age, but unless God chooses to do an Abraham and Sarah with us, that seems to be our lot. The prophetic statement of our friend, no doubt well intended, simply did not come true.

In the time I have been a Christian, there has been a dramatic rise in the culture of Christian men and women given to using the words "The Lord has told me…" as the prefix to some statement of a prophetic nature. But when you inquire, "How did the Lord speak to you—how did it happen?" the reply nearly always comes back, "I had this inner feeling or impression in my heart that this is what the Lord is saying". Our friend in fact began his prophetic statement to us with the qualifier, "I have the *distinct impression* that the Lord is telling me…".

As this relates indirectly to what I believe to be the unbiblical expression of 'feeling called', it seemed right to include a chapter on the subject of personal guidance. Again, it is hard to find biblical evidence for the often-held premise that God guides by inner impressions of the Spirit.

Impressions are… well, just that

Garry Friesen in *Decision Making and the Will of God* has a section entitled, 'Impressions are impressions'. In 'impressions', Friesen includes the still small voice, the inner voice, inward pressure, inward urging, feelings of peace, guiding impulse, inner impressions and all similar expressions, and he raises the question, "How can I tell whether these impressions are from God or some other source?" His response:

> This is a critical question. For impressions could be
> produced by any number of sources: God, Satan, an angel,
> a demon, human emotions (such as fear or ecstasy),
> hormonal imbalance, insomnia, medication, or an upset

stomach. Sinful impressions (temptations) may be exposed for what they are by the Spirit-sensitized conscience and the Word of God. But beyond that, we encounter a subjective quagmire of uncertainty…

Inner impressions are not a form of revelation. So the Bible does not invest inner impressions with authority to function as indicators of divine guidance. Impressions are real; believers experience them. But impressions are *not authoritative*. They may be useful in pointing the way to wisdom, but on the issue of their authority, impressions are just impressions. They may be "spiritual" or reflect the influence of the Spirit, but they fall short of direct revelation and thus fall short of authoritative guidance. Impressions by any other name confuse the issue and confound the believer in decision making. Impressions are still just impressions.[1]

Why do many believers feel the need to prefix certain statements with "The Lord told me…"? I would like to suggest three reasons, one good and the other two not so spiritual.

1. A desire to encourage

A prophetic message prefixed with the words "The Lord has told me…" may be given with a genuine desire to uphold and encourage the listener. In our problems with childlessness, I am sure our friend spoke to us out of a good Christian heart and wanted to lift us up. It was certainly the sort of statement we wanted to hear, but therein lies some of the problem. In my experience of listening to prophetic messages over many years, what is given is often what the receiver or the audience wants to hear. As such, it borders on a Christianized form of fortune

....

1. G Friesen, *Decision Making and the Will of God,* rev. edn, Multnomah, Colorado Springs, 2004, p. 93.

telling, with the occultist overtones that carries with it. There is a test in the Bible by which all prophecy may be judged:

> When a prophet speaks in the name of the LORD, if the word does not come to pass or come true, that is a word that the LORD has not spoken; the prophet has spoken it presumptuously. You need not be afraid of him. (Deut 18:22)

By this test, our friend's prophecy proved to be false. (As outlined before, we were later able by the gracious intervention of God to adopt a daughter, but we never have had four children, though we have had several more spiritual children—people we have helped to become God's sons and daughters—also by his grace.)

2. A desire driven by pride

When someone says, "The Lord has told me..." there may be present the less noble motive of spiritual pride and self-aggrandizement. The believer may in fact be saying, "See how spiritual and in touch with God I am. The Lord speaks directly to me. In this I may be superior to those who look to the Bible alone as their source of guidance. I have a kind of gold phone line to God, and I can converse with him directly on matters of guidance, both for myself and for others." In fact, if one has a direct line of communication with God, might it not short-circuit the need to study the Bible seriously?

3. A desire to control

The real danger emerges when the little word 'you' is added to the statement: "The Lord has told me that *you* should..." In this manner, believers may seek to manipulate the lives of those around them. If someone says this to you, it is very difficult (and even sounds rather unspiritual) to reply, "No, he didn't!" A married woman once came to me and claimed the Lord had told her to leave her husband and to marry one of the local church ministers, who was also married at the time! She had prayed about it, and as a result said she had a feeling of peace about the decision. I am not sure whether the local minister concerned had even been consulted about the matter! When she stated that the Lord had given her this permission, what could I reply except, on the basis of his already revealed will, "No, he didn't"?

RC Sproul recalls the following:

> I remember a very difficult time in my own ministry and life when the school in which I was involved as a faculty member was moving and I didn't want to go where the school was moving, and so I spent six months unemployed. The heaviest question in my life at that time was, God, what do you want me to do? I was in agony over that, praying desperately for hours every day. I had five well-intentioned, deeply spiritual close friends come to me and tell me that God told them that I was supposed to do X, Y or Z. I thought that was remarkable because the five things that the Lord told them to tell me would have had me in five different cities in five different jobs. The only thing I liked about it were the five separate salaries, but I didn't see how I was going to be in five places at the same time. Obviously, somebody didn't have the mind of Christ.[2]

This is not meant to be a chapter on the whole question of how the Christian believer may find guidance in the complexities of life. The clearest, most useful book I have read on this subject is that by Garry Friesen mentioned previously, and I highly recommend it to the serious student—I wish I had come across it earlier in my Christian walk. While it is a bit lengthy for the casual reader, I do particularly recommend chapter 8, in which he deals with the biblical passages that are often quoted in

....

2. RC Sproul, *Now, That's a Good Question!*, Tyndale, Carol Stream, 2010, p. 205.

support of the subjective view that God guides through inner impressions.

I would, however, like to make mention of two Scripture passages that are often, I believe, misunderstood and misquoted on this subject of guidance.

Guidance in the Bible?

1. He will guide you

> "I still have many things to say to you, but you cannot bear them now. When the Spirit of truth comes, he will guide you into all the truth, for he will not speak on his own authority, but whatever he hears he will speak, and he will declare to you the things that are to come." (John 16:12-13)

You can probably see why this passage is frequently quoted in the context of the subject of guidance. The Lord Jesus promises the coming of the Holy Spirit, and this Spirit will provide guidance for the disciples; he tells them "he will guide you". Also, this Spirit will help us in the difficult matter of making decisions that will affect our future, for "he will declare to you the things that are to come". Because Jesus is describing the work that the Holy Spirit does, and since that Spirit lives in our hearts by faith, then surely, it is reasoned, he is talking about some form of guidance through inner spiritual impressions and promptings.

However, I believe this is not what this text is about. Firstly, Jesus knows that the disciples are suffering from information overload. For three years he has been teaching them, mostly in parables that they have struggled to understand, and now he is in the process of giving them a long final speech at the Last Supper in the upper room. There is still much more information he wants to impart to them but, in his own words, "you cannot bear them now" (John 16:12). Yet in a few minutes' time Jesus will walk out of the door of the upper room to his arrest, trial and crucifixion. In fact, this is the last opportunity he has to teach them before his Passion. He still has "many things" to tell them, but he refrains from doing so because they are not yet ready to receive them. So the obvious questions are these: Did Jesus ever impart this additional teaching? If so, when? And if so, where can we find it?

Jesus himself answers all these questions: "When the Spirit of truth comes, he will guide you into all the truth" (John 16:13). In other words, this additional information will be given to the disciples, and through them to the church, after the day of Pentecost—after the coming of the Holy Spirit. Now the critical question remains: Where can we find this additional revelation? I believe the answer is in the epistles and later books of the New Testament.

Constantly the apostle Paul insists that his teachings and writings did not come from himself:

> For I would have you know, brothers, that the gospel that
> was preached by me is not man's gospel. For I did not
> receive it from any man, nor was I taught it, but I received
> it through a revelation of Jesus Christ. (Gal 1:11-12)

The text above from John 16 is not about inner, subjective spiritual guidance, but about *outward* objective spiritual guidance through God's fuller revelation. It is through the writings of the apostles and other authors of the later New Testament books that Jesus' extra revelation is given to the church, and as such they become a rich source of guidance to the believer who takes the time to study them.

This may also help to explain the unusual structural manner in which the New Testament is set out. If, for instance, you want to know about the facts regarding the crucifixion of our Lord—that is, about the events that transpired—you usually go to the gospels for that information. Each Gospel writer devotes up to a third of his Gospel length to focusing on just one week of Jesus' life, describing his Passion in some detail. If, however, you desire to know what the crucifixion of Jesus really means—the theology of the cross, the Christian doctrine of the atonement— then you are more directed to the epistles, particularly, say, to Romans 3 and 5, 1 Peter, or Hebrews. (The Gospel of John does also contain a number of references to the coming atonement, and of course Mark 10:45 has that wonderful summary verse: "For even the Son of Man came not to be served but to serve, and to give his life as a ransom for many".)

If you want to know what events happened on the day of the resurrection, again you go to the gospels for this information. If you wish to inquire what the resurrection means, you go over to a passage like 1 Corinthians 15 in the epistles.

To give another example, the idea of justification is presented to us in pictorial form in the parable of the Pharisee and the tax collector. "This man went down to his house *justified*, rather than the other" (Luke 18:14), Jesus teaches of the repentant taxman. But if you wish to investigate the biblical teaching on the Christian doctrine of justification by faith, then you must turn over to the epistles, in particular to Romans and Galatians. So the harder teaching, which Jesus said the disciples in the upper room were not ready to receive, we find largely in the apostolic letters. (I think most new Christians find the epistles harder to read and understand than the gospels.)

2. A change of direction

On this important subject of guidance, here is another Scripture that is often misquoted. In Acts 16, Paul and his companions have been travelling through Asia Minor (now called Turkey) on the apostle's second missionary journey. As Luke records:

> And [Paul and his companions] went through the region of Phrygia and Galatia, having been forbidden by the Holy Spirit to speak the word in Asia. And when they had come up to Mysia, they attempted to go into Bithynia, but the Spirit of Jesus did not allow them. (Acts 16:6-7)

This passage is often pointed to as an example of a normal way by which God guides his people. Twice, a door of opportunity for the gospel seems to have opened, and twice the Holy Spirit prevents them from walking through that door. Finally, Paul is given a vision of a man beseeching him to cross over the water from Asia into Europe to begin gospel work there in Macedonian Greece (Acts 16:9).

It is often assumed that Paul might have received some kind of inner guidance or subjective experience from the Holy Spirit directing him as to how he should or should not proceed. It is therefore reasoned that this is a valid example of the kind of way by which the Holy Spirit may guide us today in our daily lives and ministries, by similar inner impressions. Let me respond to this in three ways:

i) We are not given any indication in the passage as to how the Holy Spirit directed the apostle and his fellow workers. To assume that the guidance came through some kind of inner impression or a feeling of being 'called' is to read something into the passage that is not there. We simply are not told in what manner the Spirit of Jesus communicated with them.

ii) We must be careful about assuming that because the Spirit spoke to Paul in a certain manner, this is an ongoing example of how God guides today. As we have noticed previously, Paul is no ordinary Christian, and in one sense he is different even from all the other apostles. They had been with Jesus and travelled alongside him "during all the time" of his earthly ministry (Acts 1:21).

But Paul was not an apostle of that kind. He did not travel with Jesus; in fact, he was violently opposed to Jesus and the church until his dramatic conversion on the road to Damascus, after Jesus had returned to heaven. So from where did Paul get his knowledge of the gospel that he went about proclaiming? As we saw previously, over and over he insists:

> For I would have you know, brothers, that the gospel that was preached by me is not man's gospel. For I did not receive it from any man, nor was I taught it, but I received it through a revelation of Jesus Christ. (Gal 1:11-12)

Paul was given direct communication with his Lord in a manner that seems to have been unique even among the apostles. In this sense, he stands in a category of one. I think, therefore, that we must be very careful about saying, "Because the Spirit guided Paul in a certain way, this way is to be a normative experience for all Christians". Paul's experience was anything but normative.

iii) We need to understand one other distinctive feature that guided Paul's ministry and where he should or should not go. He had been personally commissioned by the Lord Jesus to be engaged purely in primary evangelism. It was Paul's guiding ministry principle not to go to places in which the gospel had already been planted by other workers. It could be that Paul had simply heard that there were other evangelists working in Bithynia and the province of Asia, and so in obedience to his commission he decided not to go there (Rom 15:20).

The Water Tower Monster

Let Friesen have the last word:

> While engaged in a ministry to high school students in eastern Oklahoma, I once began a youth meeting with the following declaration: "This afternoon, I have a message from the Water Tower Monster." I gained immediate attention as their curiosity was piqued. "The Water Tower Monster is an awesome spectre who lives beneath the water tower just outside of town beside Highway 59. His message is this: He wants everyone in town to believe in him. He says that if there are any unbelieving residents remaining at the end of one year, he will destroy the whole town. When you believe in him, you will experience an unmistakable shiver in your liver. The stronger your faith becomes, the more he will communicate with your inner being. Are there any questions?"
>
> After a few moments of restless silence, one student decided to humour me. "I live pretty close to that tower. Why haven't I ever seen this monster?"
>
> "The Water Tower Monster is only visible to believers," I replied.
>
> Another spoke up. "Then you have personally *seen* the monster with your own eyes?"
>
> "Oh, yes. Not, however, with my physical eyes. I see him with the eyes of my heart."
>
> "The eyes of your heart?"
>
> "Right. As I grow closer to the Water Tower Monster, the liver shivers become stronger and his presence is more clearly confirmed within."
>
> One boy looked especially perplexed. "Wait a minute. Are you talking about the eyes of your heart, or the eyes of your liver?"
>
> "That's right," I said.

A girl probed further. "Has anyone else ever felt these liver shivers?"

"Of course. All true believers have them."

"But how do you know the difference between a genuine 'liver shiver' and liver disease?" she continued.

"When you experience the real thing, there is no doubt about it. The inner message is as distinct as if the Water Tower Monster were speaking audibly."

"This is ridiculous!" one of the kids said, to the obvious approval of all present.

"Tell me," I replied, "is your belief in God substantially different from my 'faith' in the Water Tower Monster?"

What followed was a lively discussion of the foundation of Christian belief. And many of those young people came to appreciate more than ever that their faith was built not upon a wholly subjective foundation, but upon the solid rock of God's entrance into human history and his objective revelation to man.[3]

---

3. Friesen, pp. 89-90.

eight

WHO SHOULD GO INTO THE MINISTRY?

Commas can be misleading things. Have you ever noticed for instance that many lawyers have an aversion to commas when they are drawing up wills and other legal documents for they are often afraid that the insertion of a comma may change the meaning of the sentence and lead to further angst or litigation in order to sort out the true meaning of the statement and so legal documents may tend to ramble on rather like this sentence and be largely devoid of punctuation and I was told by a legal friend of mine that in days past lawyers used to be paid by the word?

The earliest Greek manuscripts of the New Testament suffer from a similar problem when it comes to punctuation. Not only do they have no commas; they have no punctuation at all! So if a scholar is attempting a fresh translation of the New Testament from Greek into, say, English, the scholar must make personal decisions about where the punctuation should go. Obviously, two translators may come up with slightly different solutions during this exercise, and the placement of the punctuation may make a difference to the meaning of the translated text in some places.

The situation is even more complex than this. Some years ago I took my long-suffering family along to see one of the most famous of all biblical manuscripts, the Codex Sinaiticus, on display in the British Library in London. There is quite a romantic story behind the discovery of this manuscript. A Russian Christian explorer, Count Tischendorf, made several visits beginning in 1844 to the Russian Orthodox monastery of Saint Catherine, built on the lower slopes of the supposed site of Mount Sinai. He had a particular interest in discovering old biblical manuscripts, and the obvious place to look was in very dry desert situations in which moisture may not have had the opportunity to corrupt the valuable documents. It was apparently during the last of five visits to the monastery, in 1859, that he discovered this codex. (The word 'codex' simply means it was in book form bound at the edges, rather than in the traditional scroll format.) It has been claimed that he found the book in a pile of rubbish due to be burned!

According to the *Oxford Dictionary of the Christian Church*, the so-called Sinai Codex contains the whole of the New Testament and most of the Old Testament in the Greek language, and is still considered one of the most ancient of all the major New Testament manuscripts. Most scholars date its composition at about 350-400 AD. Eventually it was moved to the Imperial Library in St Petersburg, becoming the personal possession of the Tsar of Russia. In 1933, the cash-strapped communist government sold it to the British Museum for £100,000, and from there it was later moved to the British Library, where it is a prime exhibit. It is used as a basic text in nearly all modern biblical translations.

If my family had been interested and observant, they would have noticed that it was all written in capital letters (called 'uncials'), in four narrow columns per page, not only without any punctuation, but without even any spaces between the words!

```
SOTHEDOCUMEN
THASABOUTTWE
LVELETTERSPERL
INEANDLOOKSS
OMETHINGLIKETH
ISANDYOUWILLNO
TICETHATATTHE
EDGEOFTHECOL
UMNITJUSTGOES
DOWNTOTHENEX
TLINEEVENIFINTH
EMIDDLEOFAWOR
DTHISWASPARTL
YTOSAVEVELLUM
WHICHWASVERYE
XPENSIVEPUNCTU
ATIONANDGAPSB
ETWEENTHEWOR
DSTAKEUPALOTO
FSPACEHOWEVER
IHOPEYOUNOTICE
THATONCEYOUG
ETTHEHANGOFIT
ITISACTUALLYQUI
TIEASYTOREADA
NDPUNCTUATE
```

Some wayward commas

The reason I mention all this is to confess that I was once led astray by some errant commas in an English translation from the Greek New Testament. You will recall that in my early Christian experience I was perplexed by this often-heard question: "Do you feel God is calling you into the ministry?"

By now I hope you are convinced that the concept of 'feeling called' is quite foreign to the language of the Scriptures, Old or

New Testaments. Evangelical Christians hold to the Reformation principle of 'sola scriptura': that Scripture alone is the final arbiter in all matters of Christian belief and practice. At the time of the Reformation it was felt that many medieval church traditions, practices and beliefs were contrary to the Bible and needed to be revised, reformed and in some cases discarded, on the final basis of whether or not the ancient tradition agreed with Scripture.

But this process did not end with the Reformation. The church is to be constantly reforming itself, examining its fondly held traditions, to discover whether it may again be falling into the medieval trap of elevating human traditions to be on a par with, or even superior to, the teachings of the Bible. There is nothing wrong with traditions as such, and it is impossible to avoid church traditions completely. I attend a fairly informal church, but even there we have developed our own way of doing things—our traditions if you like. But even in the most laid-back of evangelical churches, we must be constantly reviewing what we do to ensure it is as close to biblical standards as we can make it. One of the underlying assertions of this book is that some of our commonly used spiritual expressions belong more to a kind of evangelical folk religion than to the language of the Bible.

So before I explain about those wayward commas, let me first discuss the second half of the expression in this chapter's title: "into the ministry".

What does it mean to go into the ministry? How do you know if you should go into the ministry? What is the ministry? These are some of the constant questions that troubled me as I found myself surrounded by sincere believers who were regularly talking about 'feeling called', because I had not felt anything of that nature before. As I mentioned in chapter 3, when I asked my fellow students, "What does it feel like? How do you know?" I sometimes received the rather unsatisfactory rejoinder, "Oh, you will just know when it happens!"

A breakthrough for me came when studying Paul's letter to the Ephesians in its original Greek language as part of our college studies. The passage we were studying was Ephesians 4:11-13, which is so critical to this discussion that I have quoted it here in full. This translation is from the Revised Standard Version of the Bible, because this was the English text being used at our college and in most churches at that time. Discussing the gifts the risen Christ has bestowed on the church by his Spirit, the apostle Paul says:

> And his gifts were that some should be apostles, some prophets, some evangelists, and some pastors and teachers, for the equipment of the saints, for the work of ministry, for building up the body of Christ, until we all attain to the unity of the faith and of the knowledge of the Son of God, to mature manhood, to the measure of the stature of the fullness of Christ. (Eph 4:11-13, RSV)

Paul begins this section by homing in on a limited selection of the gifts of the Spirit of Christ: apostles, prophets, evangelists, pastors and teachers. Although this looks as if this is a list of five gifts, it is actually only four, since the role of pastor/teacher seems to be one entity in the Greek. A pastor must teach, and a teacher must also pastor. We should not drive a wedge between these two roles. Sometimes one may hear a church leader say, "I have been called only to teach the Bible—I do not have the time or gifts to run around pastoring people", and sometimes vice versa. It is wrong to make this dichotomy. The two *normally* must go together. You may find that you are stronger in one role than the other, but the Greek implies that you cannot opt out of one half of this particular ministry.

What do the four gifts share?

Out of the more than 20 spiritual gifts of the risen Christ that are mentioned within the New Testament, why does the apostle Paul focus on these four? What unifying quality do these particular gifts have in common?

The quality that links them together is that they all minister the word of God in different ways. The *apostles'* role was to bear witness to the ministry of Jesus, and especially as eyewitnesses to his life, death and resurrection, from the time of John the Baptist onwards. When Matthias was chosen to replace Judas after Judas hanged himself, these were precisely the qualities that were required of him (Acts 1:21-22). We say in the Creed that the church is apostolic, because it is founded upon the apostles' eyewitness testimony, both spoken and written. I believe the gift of apostleship to be the only gift of the Spirit which can be said with some certainty to have died out, since what constituted the gift was the person so gifted being an eyewitness to Jesus' ministry, especially his death and resurrection. Even the apostle-come-lately Paul could claim, "Am I not an apostle? Have I not *seen* Jesus our Lord?" (1 Cor 9:1) All of these eyewitnesses have now, of course, fallen asleep.

The term *prophets* probably refers to the Old Testament prophets, though Paul may have in view as well certain prophets of his own time. Earlier in the letter to the Ephesians, Paul has declared that the church is built upon the foundation of the apostles and prophets (Eph 2:20); that is, upon their teaching and witness. Thirdly, *evangelists*, of course, proclaim the gospel and seek to convince men and women to turn to Christ. The *pastor/ teacher* also is to preach and teach the word of God, seeking to build up the believers in their maturity and spiritual fruitfulness, usually within the fellowship of the local church.

Why does the apostle Paul focus upon these particular

spiritual roles? He is saying that the ministry of the word of God is the most important and vital of all the gifts of the Spirit, and that the continuing vibrant life of the body of Christ depends upon this particular gift being exercised effectively. If you lose a hand, you can survive and live a productive life, even compensating in part for the absent hand. But if you lose a head, there can be no compensation. If the ministry of the word of God is absent, or given low priority, then the body of Christ will atrophy and wither. Picture two churches: one has good, effective teaching from the Bible but is organizationally a bit of a shambles; the second is brilliantly administered but the Bible is neglected or even vilified. Which would you rather attend? To which would you recommend a new believer go? To which would you take your children? Having personally experienced both types, I know my answer.

Paul is not saying in any way that those who minister the word are in themselves more important than others in the church. He is declaring that these four *ministries* are the most critical and important for the ongoing health and spiritual wellbeing of the body. After all, we are all to be servants of Christ, whether leader or led; we are all in the long run unworthy workers, and our service to him should be distinguished by humility and lowliness of heart, and not by pride, arrogance, fame-seeking or empire building. Whatever gifts we have come from Christ, not from ourselves.

If those who bring us the word of God have the most vital role, what are to be their goals? As they exercise their ministries, for what practical outcomes should they be looking? According to the English translation of the Bible our theological college was using at the time, and reproduced above, it looks as if they have three roles to perform (and note the placement of the commas):

- "for the equipment of the saints,"
  The term 'saints' is the New Testament term for every Christian. Each believer is a saint, having been regenerated or born again of the Spirit of God, and daily being sanctified and becoming more like Jesus, "being transformed into the same image from one degree of glory to another" (2 Cor 3:18). Saints are not some particularly holy people who have had sainthood bestowed upon them by the church and who are often portrayed as having golden dinner plates behind their heads! Again, the Bible must have final precedence over our traditions. So the first job of those who teach the word is to equip the believers, according to this text.
- "for the work of ministry,"
  If the first role was "for the equipment of the saints", the next role appears to be to execute "the work of ministry". So it appears that the work of the ministry belongs to the leaders (the apostles, prophets, evangelists and pastor/teachers).
- "for building up the body of Christ,"
  The third role is to bring the church to maturity, seeking to make it into a strong, loving, unified body.

So, as implied by the text in the English version I was using at the time, we could express it diagrammatically like this:

Jesus' gifts were apostles, prophets, evangelists, pastors and teachers		
1 for the equipment of the saints	2 for the work of ministry	3 for building up the body of Christ

Only one quality seemed to be missing: the ability to leap over ten-storey buildings in a single bound!

As I studied the text in the original language, it occurred to me that two commas had crept into the English translation that probably had no right to be there: the comma after 'saints' and the one after 'ministry'. They were not there in the original Greek, as we have seen, and probably should not be there in the English. When we remove them, the verses read quite differently:

> And his gifts were that some should be apostles, some prophets, some evangelists, and some pastors and teachers, *for the equipment of the saints for the work of ministry and for building up the body of Christ*, until we all attain to the unity of the faith and of the knowledge of the Son of God, to mature manhood, to the measure of the stature of the fullness of Christ.

Do you see the difference? The work of those who teach us the divine word is to equip the believers so that *the believers* can do the work of ministry and build up the body of Christ. Or again, to put it diagrammatically:

Jesus' gifts were apostles, prophets, evangelists, pastors and teachers	
for the equipment of the saints	
1 for the work of ministry	2 and for building up the body of Christ

So now we are in a position to ask a very basic question from this text: to whom does the work of the ministry belong? Paul's answer is that it belongs to the saints—that is, to all the believing members of the body of Christ. One church denomination recently declared that one particular woman, long dead, is Australia's very own saint—our first. But this shows a complete disregard of the meaning of 'saint' in the New Testament. When Paul writes to the "saints in Christ Jesus who are at Philippi" (Phil 1:1), or Corinth, or Galatia, he is referring to the whole believing body—not to a small elite group of exceptional Christians who are to receive a kind of posthumous spiritual medal.

To put it another way: from the moment you became a believing Christian, you have been in the ministry. The risen Jesus has generously distributed his spiritual gifts to his church, and these ministry gifts vary enormously from person to person. In the New Testament there are several lists of the various gifts of the Spirit, and these lists may not be exhaustive in themselves. Not everyone has the gift of evangelism, or administration, or helping or encouragement or whatever. When you first become a Christian, your practical gifts may be very minimal and may need to be nurtured and developed. Both the led and the leaders need patience.

But now we need to ask a second vital question. If all believers are in the ministry from the moment they come to Christ, what is to be their purpose and goal? What are they seeking to achieve? Again we turn to the text for the answer: "building up the body of Christ". The gifts of the Spirit are to be used for the benefit of others, and are not given for a believer's own personal indulgence. Your object as a believer is to help and encourage others to become strong, mature and productive for the kingdom of God. Hopefully others will be helping you along the same path.[1]

By the way, in fairness, these two offending commas were subsequently removed from later editions of the RSV translation and omitted from subsequent translations like the New International Version:

> It was he who gave some to be apostles, some to be prophets, some to be evangelists, and some to be pastors and teachers, to prepare God's people for works of service, so that the body of Christ may be built up… (Eph 4:11-12, NIV1984)

Breakthrough

Now as I considered these things, a fresh new thought began to impress itself upon me:

> **Q:** If every believer is in the ministry from the moment he or she comes to faith in Jesus, then why was it that I had (and still have) never felt called into the ministry?
>
> **A: Because I was already in it!**

From the moment I had became a genuine believer, I had been in the ministry. A believer cannot "go into the ministry" any more than a newborn baby can go into the human race. You are in it by reason of your birth, or in this case, new birth.

This was like a breath of fresh air. The question that had

---

1. A brief word about the gift of tongues: if a person has the ability to speak in the 'tongues of men' as described in Acts 2—that is, the supernatural ability to speak the gospel in a language not known to the speaker but clearly understood by the hearer who does speak that language—then I think that miraculous gift ranks very highly. It's up there with prophecy. If you have this gift, then I think you are as close to being an apostle as a non-apostle can be. If, however, the gift being exercised is the 'tongues of angels' mentioned in 1 Corinthians 13:1, which is for personal piety and edification only, then I thinks it ranks fairly lowly in Paul's estimation, as it does not edify others (1 Cor 14:19).

so often perplexed me, of whether or not I should go into the ministry, suddenly moved from the subjective realm of some ill-defined inner prompting to a more objective position. I could begin to get a handle on it. The question was no longer "Should I go into the ministry?" That question had become a *non sequitur*—I was in the ministry whether I liked it or not, as all true believers are from conversion. The question was now "What type of ministry?" I was beginning to consider the pastor/teacher role, but did I have the kind of gifts suitable for this position? To answer this question, I could ask the opinions of others—my peers, my lecturers, and Christian leaders whose opinion I respected. I could begin to flutter my wings in pastoral ministry to see whether I had any aptitude for it.

There all the time

Now there is nothing particularly revolutionary about this. In fact, this truth had been there in the Acts of the Apostles all the time. One strategic question worth asking is this: "What difference does the day of Pentecost make? What does the church have after the day the Holy Spirit comes, that it did not possess previously?"

The first and most obvious answer is "power". After all, this is exactly what Jesus had promised to his disciples: "You will receive power when the Holy Spirit has come upon you" (Acts 1:8). It has often been pointed out that the Greek word here is not *exousia*, often translated 'power' but really meaning 'authority', but *dunamis*, from which comes English words like 'dynamo', 'dynamic' and even 'dynamite'. The frightened, reclusive disciples who fled from the garden of Gethsemane and denied any knowledge of their persecuted Lord in fear of their lives were transformed at Pentecost into men who, in time, turned the world upside down.

It was also a time of enormous spiritual expansion. The 120 disciples in the upper room on that day soon became 3000, then 5000, and then began to spread across the ancient world, beginning to fill their evangelistic nets with "a great multitude that no-one could number" (Rev 7:9).

But the central meaning of the day of Pentecost for the church is probably found in the words of the prophet Joel, which Peter quotes in his first Christian sermon that fateful day:

> And in the last days it shall be, God declares,
> that I will pour out my Spirit on all flesh,
> and your sons and your daughters shall prophesy,
> > and your young men shall see visions,
> > and your old men shall dream dreams;
> even on my male servants and female servants
> > in those days I will pour out my Spirit, and they shall
> > prophesy. (Acts 2:17-18, quoting Joel 2:28-32)

As a believer, you may never have thought of yourself as a prophet. But if you are a regenerate, born-again believer and disciple of Christ, then you are in fact a prophet. One of the roles of a prophet in the Old Testament, though not the only one, was to predict the events of the future. Every believer has the ability to do the same. Suppose, when sharing your faith, you say to someone enquiring into Christianity, "If you put your faith and trust in Jesus Christ, then when you die you will go to heaven", then you are in fact predicting the future. You are predicting something about that person's eternal condition after this life is over, in the future. You may also warn them about the dire consequences of not believing. Either way, you would be fulfilling one of the functions of a prophet: predicting the future.

You might object, "But I only told them what I read in the Bible! That does not seem to qualify me as a prophet." But why not? The prophets in the Old Testament did not invent their prophecies. Their messages were given to them by God, just as ours are, and they simply passed these messages on. The only difference between them and us is that they often received their messages verbally from God, and the messages were only later written down, whereas we receive our messages from God already written down for us. Either way, it is all prophecy.

But according to Joel, and to Peter in Acts 2, to whom is this ministry given?

In short, to "all flesh [people]" (Acts 2:17).

In the Old Testament, the Spirit of God for works of ministry was not given to all of God's people all of the time. Sometimes the Spirit of God would come upon a prophet, like Isaiah, to speak the words of God. Sometimes the Spirit would empower a person to give leadership in a battle situation, as in the book of Judges. Some of the kings of Israel, like David, were empowered by the Spirit for the role of guiding the nation (though in one case—that of Saul—the Spirit of kingship was later withdrawn). Even for artistic gifting, like that of the craftsmen who made the ornaments for the tabernacle, the Spirit was given. The impression presented to us within the pages of the Old Testament is somewhat like a scatter-gun—one here, one there, but never to all of the people all of the time.

But after Pentecost, the Spirit is given to "all flesh"—that is, to all of God's people, all of the time. Lest we miss the point, God's word spells it out in greater detail:

- From now on, there will be no distinction as far as gender is concerned. The Spirit is poured out on "your sons and your daughters".
- There will be no distinction as regards age: "your young men shall see visions, and your old men shall dream dreams".

- There will be no distinction as regards social status. The gifting of the Spirit will fall across the classes, from low to high born: "even on my male servants and female servants… I will pour out my Spirit".
- There will be no distinction as regards race. Peter hints that this pouring out, at that time confined to the Jewish followers, will be further extended to the Gentiles: "you will receive the gift of the Holy Spirit. For the promise is for you and for your children [the Jews] and for all who are far off [the Gentiles]" (Acts 2:38-39).

In the verses from Ephesians 4 that I have discussed in this chapter, Paul is simply repeating the principle laid down on the day of Pentecost: all of God's people—the saints—are in the ministry, all of the time, from the first moment they come to faith in Jesus. You and I cannot 'go' into the ministry, any more than we can 'go' into the human race once we have been born. Once we are born again, we are in the ministry of Christ, full time, together, whether we want to be or not. And it is a great honour and privilege.

One question, however, still troubled me. If all the saints are in the ministry, why do we call some people 'minister' or 'pastor' and pay them for their particular service? Also, what motivates a person to want to take up this role of church leader in the first place? If we have excluded a 'felt call' from the equation, then what motivation remains?

The Pastoral Epistles would soon yield a seemingly very unspiritual answer to this question.

nine

LEARNING THE HARD WAY

"And why do you want to come sailing with me?"

Soon after I began studying at my new college, one of the other students came to me and asked, "Would you be willing to come as a leader on a Christian sailing camp?" Now at this stage I had virtually no experience in any form of public Christian ministry, apart from teaching a few Sunday School lessons I had been asked to give during the time when I was not even a Christian! As for sailing, my experience was even less, at zero. I do not think I had ever been in any form of sailing boat! But I was desperate for experience, so I said "Yes".

Let me share with you all I have learned about sailing from this experience.

Should you want to change direction when you are sailing into the wind, the procedure is fairly simple. It is called 'tacking'. You are sailing along at about 45 degrees to the direction of the wind. The mainsail is a triangle attached to the mast along its leading edge, with its bottom edge attached to a hunk of timber aptly called the 'boom'. One end of the boom is attached to the bottom of the mast, as low as is practicable (more of that later!), with a swivel kind of thing that allows it to swing freely. The free end of the boom has a rope attached to it onto which the 'captain' holds grimly, trying to keep its unruly behaviour under control. In front of the mast there is usually a smaller triangular sail called a 'jib'.

When you are going into the wind, all is fairly straightforward. The boat, the mainsail and the jib are in a sort of straight line, and the boom sits more or less over the centre of the boat, as I recall. In fact, the harder the leader can pull the boom in, the faster the boat goes, which is great fun.

To change direction, the boat is simply turned deliberately into the wind. The sail flaps wildly for a few seconds as the wind goes equally down both sides of it. The boat loses speed for a moment, but as soon as the momentum of the turn passes the 'straight into the wind' point, the sail begins to fill again on the other side, and away you go in a different direction. The boom moves at a leisurely pace from one side of the boat to the other, and the crew members simply duck their heads under it and move to the new windward side of the boat. No problems.

But let us imagine that you want to change direction while going downwind. This is called 'jibing', and it is something else again.

When sailing with the wind behind you, the boom sticks out at right angles to the boat, in order to catch the most wind from behind. If one is very skilful, and the wind is blowing almost exactly from behind, you can do a clever thing. If the mainsail is on, say, the right-hand side (starboard?), you can put the jib up on the left side so that it is receiving the wind directly, without the mainsail stealing its wind. The jib is held out in this position by a stick kind of thing. In a good wind the boat can go quite fast in this position, but it is somewhat unstable as you can imagine with this lump of timber hanging over the side.

Now, please follow this carefully. To change direction, with the mainsail and the boom on, let us say, the right-hand side, you turn the boat deliberately to the right. If you do this far enough, the boat is now more or less broadside on to the direction of the wind, and the boom is now pointing straight into the wind. The mainsail begins to flap with an unnerving ferocity as the wind goes equally down both sides of it.

Again, the momentum of the turn takes the boat past this critical point, and the boom suddenly decides it has an urgent need to be on the left-hand side of the vessel. It crosses the centre of the boat at the speed of a Boeing 747 at lift-off. All who do not hit the deck as this express train crosses over will be decapitated! I think any sailor who does this sort of thing should be issued with the kind of helmet worn by American football players.

One day in precisely this situation, as the responsible leader, I yell out, "Hit the decks, boys, or we're all dead men! Panic! Down! Everyone dive!" (It was cool-headed captaincy like this that endeared Nelson to his sailors.)

I forgot to mention one small point. If the sail is on the right side of the boat, then the crew must be on the left side to balance the weight of the boom and the pressure of the wind on the sail. So at this particular moment, the crew is on the left side of the boat as we start to change direction. Two seconds later, the boom is now also on the left side, filling with wind, and the crew, at my instructions, has hit the deck—on the left side. All the weight is now on the wrong side of the boat. At this point the mast decides it has had enough of this foolishness and wants to lie flat down in the water for a rest. The crew now tries to scramble from the left side to the right, seeking to convince the mast not to do this. If one is very athletic and fit, one can actually throw oneself over the side of the boat, holding grimly onto the side-rail if there is one. If you are extremely fit, or just stupid, you can actually dangle so far overboard that you find yourself standing on the keel of the boat (the wing sort of thing that sticks down like the inverted tail of a plane, and is supposed to stop this sort of thing from happening). While all this is going on, I (the 'captain') am desperately hanging onto the rope attached to the end of the boom, seeking to bring its wild gyrations under some kind of control, and secretly begging it not to join the mast in this mutiny.

But more is to follow. You will recall that at this critical moment we are broadside on to the wind. Once the mast has won its bid to lie down in the water (which it usually did with me), the upturned hull of the boat acts as a kind of sail, with the wind pushing the crippled boat along. The mast, which has toppled over downwind, is now leading this procession.

As the sail fills with water, the mast begins to sink under the weight. The lake we are sailing on is quite shallow, so eventually the top of the mast digs into the muddy bottom. At this moment I discover that metal masts are usually hollow to save weight, so now the hollow mast begins to fill up with mud.

There is an authorized procedure for righting a capsized craft, but it does not apply in this situation. The other leaders come out in an outboard motor, all grinning from ear to ear, and drag us ignominiously back to the shore. The crew members, all wearing life-jackets, seem to have survived but do not thank me for the afternoon's entertainment.

On this camp I never did really get the hang of jibing. But as the camp progressed, I noticed I was becoming quite popular, and boys were actually asking to go sailing with me. When at last I asked one why he volunteered to join my crew, he replied, "I have to go for my Capsize Certificate!"

You might be asking, "What has all this got to do with ministry?" This camp was my first introduction to any organized form of Christian ministry. Each day there were devotions for the boys, some of whom were not believing Christians, and every evening the leaders took it in turns to give a talk on the gospel and the way of salvation. There was no undue pressure, and from memory, some of the boys indicated they wanted to follow Jesus. However, having observed my sailing skills, the other leaders did not ask me to give one of the talks.

Trial and error

At the end of the same year, the same fellow college student asked me to come as a leader on something called a 'beach mission'. Some people never learn. Having not the foggiest idea what a 'beach mission' was, again I replied in the affirmative.

We all lived in tents for about ten days at Palm Beach, Sydney, and ran daily fun and Bible-based programs for children, youth and adults. On the Sunday evening we were scheduled to have a campers' church service, and the leader who had invited me asked me to give the main talk. He must not have been aware that I had never given a Christian address in public in my life!

A large number of people of all ages turned up. My feeling was that I should aim the message at the children but make the talk strong enough so that the adults would be able to relate to it as well. From memory, the event went quite well, and the team members were very encouraging. I found I had a bit of a talent for giving children's talks.

The next year I was back at the sailing camp, and this time I was asked to give one of the main evening talks to the boys. After my input, those who wanted to find out more about following Jesus were invited to come to one of the tents where I could talk personally with them. Although I half expected no-one to come, one ginger-haired teenager turned up. We spent some time in discussion, and I prayed with him. Some decades later, I met him again for the first time since the camp. He had slightly less ginger hair, a wife and family, and was pastor of a Christian church. I like to think my input, by God's grace, may have been a small link along the way.

Now I do not want to argue from personal experience, for in the long run—to repeat the Reformation dictum—the Scriptures are our final benchmark in all matters of Christian belief and practice. As the official doctrinal statement of one denomination puts it:

> Holy Scripture contains all things necessary to salvation; so that whatever is not read in Scripture, nor may not be proved from it, is not to be imposed upon any person that it should be believed as essential to the faith, nor should it be taught as required and necessary for salvation. (My paraphrase.)

However, I hope my early experience illustrates the practical process by which I believe spiritual gifts are usually discovered and developed. Spiritual gifts are not, by and large, discovered in a vacuum. You do not discover your ministry gifting by sitting in a dark room vowing not to move until God tells you what to do. I am in no way denying that God could, if he wished, write a message to you on the wall with a finger as he did in Daniel's time, or speak directly and audibly to you as he did to Samuel, but from my observation and enquiries these days that is not the usual way it happens. To use the very old illustration, the handles on a bicycle are only useful if the bicycle is actually moving. Sitting in the garage, they are quite useless.

Normally, spiritual gifts are discovered as you leave your comfort zone and propel yourself into situations of ministry, which may even prove to be somewhat threatening. I believe there is a degree of trial and error in the process, guided at all times by God's word, and bearing in mind that God has chosen to use "jars of clay" (2 Cor 4:7).

I am surprised at how many believers I meet who are looking and waiting for a personal visitation from an angel or even Jesus, in some form, before they are willing to venture out into practical ministry. Our Lord, however, told his disciples, "A little while, and you will see me no longer..." (John 16:16).

I know our Lord did reveal himself to Saul-soon-to-become-Paul after Jesus' ascension back to heaven; and I have heard (and have no reason to disbelieve) stories of people who live in countries in which Christianity is largely forbidden receiving such personal revelations. But in the West, where Bibles, churches, Christian books and teaching are so freely available, to hold out for such a personal visitation seems to me to be bordering upon what the Bible calls an evil generation seeking for signs (Matt 12:38-39) and putting God to the test.

By the way, on the second sailing camp I did manage to master downwind jibing—after a fashion.

ten

A HUMAN DESIRE

Imagine you have just been asked to be the pastor of a brand new church. The church has been planted and evangelized by someone else who has since moved on to another field, and you have been left holding the ecclesiastical baby.

For starters you do not have a building to meet in, nor will the government of the day allow you to have one. You have only one copy of the Scriptures, a handwritten copy of the Old Testament possibly purchased at great expense from who knows where. Most of the New Testament epistles have not yet been written, and the four gospels have not been penned at this stage. All of your congregation members are first generation Christians, brand new converts, and until recently most of them had never even heard of Jesus. There is no church denomination to advise you as to what you should do. There are no 'how to grow a church' manuals available, no song or hymn books, no Bible colleges, no theological confessions, no notice boards, no internet, no Apostles' Creed, no Christian books of any kind. Furthermore, the congregation you have been handed is a rough-hewn lot upon whom sanctification has unevenly begun to take hold.

What would you do?

For a start, how would you decide who, if anyone, should lead?

Most of the newly founded churches mentioned in the Acts

of the Apostles, initially brought to birth by Paul or one of the other early apostolic evangelists, were in exactly this bereft position, though the situation gradually improved as the New Testament Scriptures came to be written and began to circulate more freely around the Mediterranean world and beyond. Eyewitnesses of the gospel events also travelled from church to church preaching and teaching what they had "seen" and "heard" (1 John 1:1). The *Pax Romana* (ensuring ease of travel between countries via both the Mediterranean Sea and Roman roads and the lack of customs barriers between countries) aided a reasonably quick dissemination of gospel information to the infant congregations.

When we come to this strategic subject of Christian leadership, I mentioned previously that there are parts of the New Testament that are of the utmost importance, grouped together under the general heading of the Pastoral Epistles. Most of the letters in the New Testament are written to individual churches, such as the one to the church in Ephesus, or to groups of churches, such as the epistle to the Galatians. However, there is a smallish group of letters that are written to individual Christian leaders. This group of epistles, which is often entitled the Pastoral Epistles, comprises three such letters: 1 Timothy, 2 Timothy and Titus. These three documents are of immense value in our understanding of the nature of Christian leadership, particularly within the body we call the local church.

In these letters, the apostle Paul writes to two Christian friends who are now responsible for giving leadership within new first-generation local church situations. These men, Timothy and Titus, are dealing mostly with new believers, meeting within a fellowship of churches that have only been in existence for a short time, perhaps a few years or even months.

They are trying to be God's people in situations in which no church has ever existed before. There are virtually no previous ground rules to go by. Who should be in charge? Who, if anyone, should take the lead? Should there be any leadership, or should each individual believer do his or her own thing? Or is the church to be a democratic institution along Athenian lines, in which decisions are made according to how the majority votes?

What is to be the nature of Christian leadership?

I am struggling to find a word.

If all Christians are in the ministry, as outlined previously, from the time of conversion onwards, to minister the various gifts that the risen Christ has generously distributed to all his people; and if these gifts are not for personal edification and self-aggrandizement but rather are servant gifts with which we are to encourage and help other believers to grow; and if each believer is therefore in full-time ministry from the beginning of Christian life until it finds its fulfilment in heaven; then what word are we to use for persons who give up normal means of employment to devote themselves without distraction to their particular ministries? We usually describe such people as going into 'full-time' ministry, but we have seen that this is not a wholly appropriate term, as all believers are in 'full-time' ministry from the moment of conversion.

We are usually talking here about pastors, ministers, missionaries and others who may go into what are often called para-church Christian enterprises, like, for instance, working with students on a university campus.

For want of a better word, we will refer to this group from now on as undertaking 'career' ministries (you may be able to come up with a more appropriate term). In other words, some believers decide to give up normal secular means of employment as a means of putting bread on the table, so as to be able to devote themselves more consistently to gospel work without the distraction of having to give the bulk of each working day to a secular employer.

Of course, the line between the career Christian and the ordinary full-time believer is always, by definition, blurred. Some churches, for instance, may not be able to afford to pay a pastor a full salary, and the pastor may need to supplement this income with some secular employment. Other Christians may begin in secular employment, then undertake career ministry for a while before returning to secular work. Also, many Christians who are in secular employment give themselves unstintingly to the Lord's work in their spare time, sometimes working harder than some career ministers. By 'career minister', then, we mean a person who sets aside normal means of secular employment for the sake of being more fully devoted to gospel work, and who usually is supported financially in this work by other believers.

The New Testament is not against this concept:

> Let the elders who rule well be considered worthy of double honour, especially those who labour in preaching and teaching. For the Scripture says, "You shall not muzzle an ox when it treads out the grain", and, "The labourer deserves his wages." (1 Tim 5:17-18)

We have seen previously that the ministry of the word of God is supremely vital for the wellbeing of any church. If we lack other gifts in our church, the church may be able to compensate for this lack. But if the word of God is ineffectually taught, then the church can go in only one spiritual direction.

We consider this ministry of the word to be so vital and important that we say to some people, "We would like you to give up secular employment, so that you can devote yourself to the vital dual ministries of teaching and pastoring in our church".

We usually will encourage those people to go off for a while to Bible or theological college to become more fully equipped for the task. Again, this does not mean that the pastor or minister is in any way more important than the rest of the congregation. In fact, Jesus exhorts leaders not to set themselves above other believers. They are not to wear fancy long robes; they are not to take on board impressive titles like 'Teacher', and especially not 'Father'. (Do you think Jesus may have included 'Reverend' in his list, if it had been in common use in his day?) They are not to promote themselves above their brethren (Matt 23:5-12).

Which brings us back to our fundamental question. What is it that motivates a person to undertake this kind of career ministry? If it is not 'feeling called', then what?

One day I was reading through the Pastoral Epistles and my attention was seriously arrested by this statement: "If anyone aspires to the office of overseer, he desires a noble task" (1 Tim 3:1).

We will see in a moment that the term 'overseer' is commonly used in the New Testament for a local church leader—someone who has oversight of a church congregation. Notice there is no mention of subjective call here: he "aspires to" (or 'sets his heart on') and he "desires" this particular ministry. These are desires that come from the human heart. The apostle Paul seems to be saying (with approval!) that the primary reason a person undertakes any ministry, and a career ministry in particular, is simply that the believer wants or desires to serve the Lord in this way.

Now, that sounds so unspiritual that some readers may choose to close this book at this point. However, let me immediately add this qualification: just because a believer desires a position of leadership is not enough justification in itself for the person to be given it. This desire must be *rightly motivated* and also *rightly tested*, and this testing must come from others—particularly from those who are more mature in the Christian faith. We will come back to this point in a moment.

Two key words

The New Testament in general and the Pastoral Epistles in particular use two main terms to describe a person who is to give leadership within the local church. The first term is *episkopos*, which is literally translated as 'overseer'—one who is to have oversight of the work of the gospel within the local church portion of the body of Christ. The second term is *presbuteros*, usually translated in English by the term 'elder'. 'Elder' does not necessarily mean the person is chronologically old, but refers to Christian maturity. Charles Spurgeon, for instance, became a church elder and overseer while only in his late teens. The New Testament on several occasions uses these two words interchangeably.

For instance, in Acts 20:17 we are told that "From Miletus [Paul] sent to Ephesus and called the *elders* of the church to come to him". When these elders arrived, knowing this would be the last time he would see them in this life, Paul exhorted them, finishing like this, "Pay careful attention to yourselves and to all the flock, in which the Holy Spirit has made you *overseers*…" (Acts 20:28). You will notice that the same church leaders are called both 'elders' and overseers'. Notice also the pastoral image in which the congregation at Ephesus is called a 'flock', brought together by the life-changing activity of the Holy Spirit.

At another time, writing to Titus concerning church leadership, Paul again says,

> This is why I left you in Crete, so that you might put what remained into order, and appoint *elders* in every town as I

directed you—if anyone is above reproach, the husband of one wife, and his children are believers and not open to the charge of debauchery or insubordination. For an *overseer*, as God's steward, must be above reproach. He must not be arrogant or quick-tempered or a drunkard or violent or greedy for gain, but hospitable, a lover of good, self-controlled, upright, holy, and disciplined. (Titus 1:5-8)

Again, the two terms 'elder' and 'overseer' are used interchangeably.

And even the apostle Peter, the rock upon which Jesus said he would build his church, is not too self-important to call himself an elder:

So I exhort the *elders* among you, as a fellow elder… *shepherd* the flock of God that is among you, exercising *oversight*… (1 Pet 5:1-2)

A leader within the church is to be a mature Christian, and has the God-given responsibility of giving direction to the affairs of the church. 'Elder' describes his maturity and 'overseer' embraces his function, along with the pastoral emphasis on being a 'shepherd of God's flock'.

Within the first hundred years of church history, however, the term 'overseer' became separated from that of 'elder'. 'Overseer' came to be the title used for a bishop—a person who had oversight of a group of churches, or an ecclesiastical diocese. (We see signs of this change in the letters of Ignatius, written about 100 AD on his way to martyrdom for the faith. Rather than submission to Christ or to the now fully composed Scriptures, Ignatius stresses submission to the local bishop as the touchstone for Christian unity.)

'Elder', then, was reserved for a local church pastor or minister. But *every church* described in the New Testament was a self-governing entity ruled by elders who were also overseers, and the New Testament knows nothing of 'bishops'. For instance, consider Paul's first missionary journey in which he evangelized the area of southern Asia Minor called Galatia. After he returns to his 'headquarters' at Antioch, the third-largest city in the Roman Empire, he does not write to the new churches and say, "From now on you are to take directions from the Bishop of Antioch (or from the Bishop of Galatia)". There is not the slightest hint of this in Galatians or in any other of his epistles. Whether such a development in later church structure was inevitable or even a good thing is not our object here. Perhaps you will find this a good topic for discussion.[1]

On several occasions in these three short epistles, the apostle Paul sets out in some detail the qualifications to be looked for when seeking to appoint new oversight within the church. The main passages are 1 Timothy 3:1-7 and 5:19-20, 2 Timothy 4:1-5 and Titus 1:5-9. (2 Timothy is an especially emotive letter and is infused with a unique urgency, as it is almost certainly the last letter Paul ever wrote while awaiting execution during the persecution against Christians instigated by the Emperor Nero.)

....

1. St Jerome (c. 342-420 AD), translator of the Bible into Latin, agreed that 'elder' (*presbuteros*) and 'bishop' (*episkopos*) described in fact the same person in the New Testament, and gave an interesting reason for the later separation of the terms into two differing roles:

> Hence a presbyter is the same as a bishop, and before ambition came into religion, by the prompting of the devil, and people began to say: "I belong to Paul; I to Apollo; I to Cephas", the churches were governed by the direction of the presbyters, acting as a body. But when each presbyter began to suppose that those whom he had baptized belonged to him, rather than to Christ, it was decreed in the whole church that one of the presbyters would be chosen to preside over the others, and that the whole responsibility for the church should devolve on him, so that the seeds of schism should be removed.

St Jerome, 'Commentary on the Epistle to Titus', 1:1, 5; quoted in Henry Bettenson, *The Later Christian Fathers*, Oxford University Press, London, 1970, p. 189.

I will focus on the first of these passages:

> The saying is trustworthy: If anyone aspires to the office
> of overseer, he desires a noble task. Therefore an overseer
> must be above reproach, the husband of one wife, sober-
> minded, self-controlled, respectable, hospitable, able
> to teach, not a drunkard, not violent but gentle, not
> quarrelsome, not a lover of money. He must manage his
> own household well, with all dignity keeping his children
> submissive, for if someone does not know how to manage
> his own household, how will he care for God's church? He
> must not be a recent convert, or he may become puffed up
> with conceit and fall into the condemnation of the devil.
> Moreover, he must be well thought of by outsiders, so that
> he may not fall into disgrace, into a snare of the devil.
> (1 Tim 3:1-7)

Now at the risk of being tedious, let me reiterate the fact that nowhere in the Pastoral Epistles, nor anywhere in his other letters, does Paul say, "If you are looking for someone to exercise a leadership position within the church, make sure that person feels a strong sense of calling from God." Nowhere! This language is totally foreign to the vocabulary of the New Testament.

What kind of language does the apostle use? He begins this important section in this way: "If anyone *aspires to* the office of overseer, he *desires* a noble task". Here is someone who wants to be given a position of leadership in the church. He wants it. In fact, other translations say that he "sets his heart" on the position. (I am using the masculine 'he' here reflecting the apostle's own use. Whether women should be elders in the church is not a topic pursued in this book.)

Now Paul sees nothing wrong with this in itself. He does not say, "Such a person is obviously unqualified for the role, seen by the fact that he covets the position. Anyone who promotes himself in this way is clearly not the sort of person we want!" In fact, Paul seems to be giving qualified approval to the person's desire when he adds, "he desires a noble task". As it is a noble position, it cannot be in itself ignoble to want to do it. To want to be an elected representative is not a bad thing, if your motivation is to serve the people of your constituency. If your desire is to make your name famous, to accumulate power over others or even to win a large superannuation payout, then such a desire should be rejected. It all depends on the motivation.

Two qualifications

As mentioned before, the desire to be involved in Christian ministry is a human desire upon which a person 'sets his heart'. But this desire is not, in itself, sufficient reason for a believer to be given leadership responsibility. The applicant must also be *rightly motivated* and *rightly tested*. Let us look at each of these in turn.

1. He must be rightly motivated for ministry

The example of Hudson Taylor, which we looked at earlier, is probably an excellent model of right Christian motivation. You may recall that I distilled six factors in Taylor's life that propelled him into a lifetime of dedicated service in China:

- **Environment**
  Hudson Taylor had the significant advantage of being nurtured in a godly, prayerful family, who were members of a Bible-teaching evangelical church. Now although this is a huge head start for any believer, it is not an *essential* requirement. Many Christian pastors, missionaries and leaders, this author included, have come from families where Christ is not properly honoured. A Christian upbringing is not essential, but it is a big plus.

- **Conversion**

  There used to be an Anglican bishop from these parts who was heard to say, quite openly and bravely, something like, "I have been a bishop for ten years and a Christian for only five!" A genuine conversion to faith in Christ crucified and risen, marked by a heartfelt conviction of sin and a sincere life-altering repentance, should be a leadership 'given'. Sadly, this is not always the case.

- **Gospel consequences**

  The gospel is wonderfully positive, "the power of God for salvation" (Rom 1:16); but the narrow gate leads to life, and the broad one to "destruction" (Matt 7:13-14). The risen Lord will divide the sheep from the goats on the last day, one group destined for his unending heaven, the other for where "the fire is not quenched" (Mark 9:48). A loving leader will first of all hold out and freely offer the balm of sins forgiven—the certainty, in Christ, of eternal glory and myriad other positive benefits flowing from following Jesus. But if he does not warn of the 'wrath to come', then he is like Ezekiel's watchman who fails to sound the alarm (Ezek 3:17-18), and his ministry will be blunted at best and cowardly at worst.

- **Compassion**

  Unless your heart is deeply moved by a compassion for people, and unless you are inwardly gripped by that which motivated Jesus—"When he saw the crowds, he had compassion for them, because they were harassed and helpless, like sheep without a shepherd" (Matthew 9:36)—then ministry leadership is not for you. If your desire is for position, or fame, or praise, or making a name for yourself; or if compassion for people is significantly lacking in your spiritual make-up, then I would think you are not yet ready for Christian leadership in any form.

- **Action**

When Jesus met with the woman at the well (John 4:6-42), he had at hand a number of valid excuses for not speaking with her: he seemed to be in a hurry (Samaria was a short cut to Galilee that most Jews avoided); he was weary (v. 6); he was thirsty (v. 7); he was hungry (v. 8); she was a Samaritan (despised and avoided by orthodox Jews); she was a woman (it was often frowned upon for a man to speak to a woman in public); she had a reputation (v. 17); and it ran counter to Jesus' declared policy of not taking the gospel to the Samaritans or Gentiles at this stage (Matt 10:5).

We can always find reasons close at hand for not being effectively involved in ministry. Even "I must spend more time with my family", though a very Christian thing to do, I have sometimes heard overused as a cop-out plea.

But Jesus takes action, and even finds two extra days to spend with the despised Samaritan villagers (v. 40). We can always find time for the things we really want to do.

To anyone requesting a Christian leadership position, one of the first questions should be, "What has been your experience in ministry so far, and what are you doing at the moment?"

- **Suitability**

A desire for spiritual leadership and ministry is not enough in itself. Paul says this desire must be tested by others (1 Tim 3:1-7). He sets out a series of spiritual tests by which the person who desires to be a leader may be properly assessed; and this brings us to the second requirement regarding one seeking ministry responsibility.

2. He must be rightly tested for ministry

Paul begins this section with a kind of umbrella statement: "Therefore an overseer must be above reproach…" (1 Tim 3:2). What does this mean in more practical detail? The apostle outlines a number of tests that need to be applied:

- **His family life is to be tested**

  > Therefore an overseer must be… the husband of but one wife… (3:2)

  > He must manage his own household well, with all dignity keeping his children submissive, for if someone does not know how to manage his own household, how will he care for God's church? (3:4-5)

  In Roman society it was quite common for a man to have a wife and a mistress or mistresses; in Greek society it was considered quite acceptable to have homosexual relations as well; and in some parts, having more than one wife was not frowned upon, King Herod the Great being an example. But the Christian leader is to set the congregation a model based upon Adam and Eve from one end of the Bible, and Christ and the church from the other.

- **His moral life must be tested**

  > Therefore an overseer must be… sober-minded, self-controlled, respectable, hospitable… not a drunkard, not violent but gentle, not quarrelsome, not a lover of money. (3:2-3)

- **His ability to teach must be tested**

  > Therefore an overseer must be… able to teach… (3:2)

  Recently the church I attend was searching for a new pastor. The church elders rightly went to hear the applicants teach, and in the case of those applying from overseas the elders requested several recordings of talks and sermons. In our electronic age, this is more easily done than a century ago. I am saddened to hear of pastors being appointed whose teaching ability has not even been considered.

- **His maturity must be tested**

> He must not be a recent convert, or he may become
> puffed up with conceit and fall into the condemnation of
> the devil. (3:6)

As stated previously, the term 'elder' does not necessarily refer to a person's chronological age. Grey hair does not always signify wisdom. 'Elder' refers to spiritual maturity. There have been occasions when new Christians have been unwisely thrown into frontline positions, usually with sad consequences for both the church and the individual. One person I know, who was wonderfully converted out of a gangland background, was heard to say, "I think I should go to Bible college". But church leaders immediately insisted on promoting their prize convert into ministry with young offenders, which ministry finally blew up with sad consequences. I think the new convert had it right.

- **His past must be tested**

> He must be well thought of by outsiders, so that he may
> not fall into disgrace, into a snare of the devil. (3:7)

This is a rather difficult statement, as many Christian leaders may have been converted out of a wild or sinful background, as in the famous story of Augustine of Hippo, honestly detailed in his *Confessions*. Like Augustine, they have been led to genuine and heartfelt repentance by the grace of God and, in time, have been embraced rightly into positions of Christian leadership. I think Paul means here that the potential leader should have no skeletons in the closet, no serious lapses that may relate to his time since becoming a Christian. The media love stories of pastors who are found to have had affairs when ministering some years previously, or have abused children in their charge. The ensuing publicity is never a plus for the gospel.

Why be involved in ministry?

I have been saying that if you are a believing Christian, born again of God's Spirit, then you are in full-time ministry from the moment you come to Christ until the moment you depart this life to be with him. The nature of this ministry will vary greatly according to the spiritual gifts God has given you—and he has given them to you. You must not say, "He has not given me any gifts". I have also been saying that usually you will discover your gifts by trial and error, rather than by some rarely given special revelation.

But you may still reply, "Why should I be involved in ministry? After all, I have my eternal salvation, and in the long run that is all that matters. Why can't I just coast through life until that day turns up?" I cannot believe you would sincerely say something like that, but the best answer I can give is in what motivated Paul:

> For the love of Christ controls us, because we have concluded this: that one has died for all, therefore all have died; and he died for all, that those who live might no longer live for themselves but for him who for their sake died and was raised. (2 Cor 5:14-15)

eleven

WHERE FROM HERE?

The only people who make mistakes are people who attempt to do things. If you never want to make a mistake, never want to be the object of criticism, then never do anything. The easiest role to play in the world is the role of the 'sideline critic', the 'Devil's advocate'—the one who stands at a distance smugly assessing the work of others and pointing out their obvious faults to whoever will listen, but who actively contributes little or nothing.

The gospel does not allow us to be armchair supervisors. From the moment you and I come to faith in Jesus, we are in the ministry whether we want to be or not. We serve a gracious and loving but hard taskmaster who, according to several of his parables, is looking for a return on his investment—"thirtyfold and sixtyfold and a hundredfold" (Mark 4:20).

I wish to encourage you into ministry, now, today. You should not be sitting back waiting for some supernatural visitation before you will attempt action for the kingdom of God. It is not that God cannot give you a dramatic and life-changing personal sign. God can do anything he likes, obviously. He could give you a burning bush, or a voice in the night, or a finger writing on the wall, or a blinding light, or a thousand different signs. But in my experience, and from talking to others in Christian ministry, generally he does not—at least not in countries in which Bibles, churches, courses and a mountain of useful resources are so freely available. If we are too lazy to study our Bibles, too spiritually slack to investigate the revelation he has already given us so freely, why should we expect special treatment and visitations from God? Is this what the writer of the epistle to the Hebrews implies in his opening verses?

> Long ago, at many times and in many ways, God spoke to our fathers by the prophets, but in these last days he has spoken to us by his Son, whom he appointed the heir of all things, through whom also he created the world. (Heb 1:1-2)

And he continues, in rebuke:

> For though by this time you ought to be teachers, you need someone to teach you again the basic principles of the oracles of God. You need milk, not solid food... (Heb 5:12)

You were called into the sacred ministry the moment you entered the kingdom of God. You do not need to wait for another supernatural call.

As far as the call of God is concerned, the biblical evidence is that we are called by the Spirit to do two things. First, we are called to be Christians, to follow Jesus our master all the days of our lives. Second, we are called to become holy, or to put it in simpler terms, to become more and more like Jesus. If we accept these two critical callings, and if we are actively and genuinely pursuing them, then I believe the rest of the jigsaw—questions about the future—will fall into place in God's good time.

In the meantime, we need to roll up our sleeves and get on with the job at hand.

What you attempt will vary according to the gifts and abilities Jesus has given you. There are three types of gifts that you bring to your efforts to serve Christ:

- **Gifts you had before becoming a Christian**

  If you were a good musician when you first found Christ, it stands to reason that you will probably bring this gift to the foot of his cross. You will devote it to his work. Before coming to Christ you may have had organizational abilities or personal relationship skills, which the Spirit of Christ can turn and develop for gospel work. However, you may not be limited to these 'natural gifts'...

- **Gifts you develop after coming to Christ**

  I had a friend who was a sheep farmer in New Zealand and had received only a limited education. The death of his wife resulted in his coming to faith in Jesus. After his conversion, he discovered he had an exceptional ability in languages, even topping the Wycliffe Bible Translators linguistic school he attended. In the middle and later years of his life he and his second wife translated the Bible into an aboriginal language in the far north of Australia.

  This is a story heard over and over. Believers end up in ministries they could not have foreseen; had you told them before they came to Christ that they would be doing these ministries, they would have laughed in your face. Take Peter the fisherman, for starters.

- **Gifts you are forced to develop**

  Sometimes you will find yourself in a situation in which there may be a desperate spiritual need, and no-one else able to take it on. Moses protested his inability to speak publicly, but spent the next 40 years doing so. Paul, the "Hebrew of Hebrews" (Phil 3:5), was given the life-long job of talking only to Gentiles. Sometimes you just need to apply yourself to a ministry because there is simply no alternative; there is no-one else.

The one thing you must not do is to sit on your hands until you 'feel called'. The Bible does not allow us this luxury.

WHY WE MUST STOP CALLING CHRISTIAN LEADERS 'PRIEST'

In this book, we have looked closely at the 'call of God', and tried to dispel (successfully I hope) the myths and misunderstandings that have surrounded this important biblical idea.

However, there are two other words often associated with Christian ministry that have also been causing confusion with Christian ranks for centuries. Before finishing, we should spend some time trying to untangle them.

These two words are 'priest' and 'elder'.

Priest

In the Greek New Testament, the word for 'priest' is *hiereus*. This word is used of Zechariah (father of John the Baptist) in Luke 1:5, and throughout the New Testament to refer to this special group of men (for all priests in the Bible are male). There is a similar word, *arch-hiereus*, which is used for the high priest or chief priest as, for instance, in Luke 22:54. By interchanging the *arch* part and the *hiereus* part, we end up with the English word 'hierarchy'.

Moses' brother, Aaron, was appointed by God to be the first high priest within the nation of Israel, as described in the latter chapters of Exodus. From that time onwards, for any man to be a priest in Israel, he had to be able to prove that he was physically descended from the family line of Aaron. The family name 'Cohen' is well known to many within the Western world, and this name Cohen is derived from the Hebrew word for 'priest'. Anyone with the name Cohen can claim to be descended from Aaron, the first high priest, and to be a member of a unique and highly regarded group within the history of the nation of Israel. So *hiereus* is the Greek word for priest in the New Testament, and 'Cohen' is derived from the Old Testament Hebrew word.

If a person was an *hiereus* it meant he was appointed by God to act as a mediator between God and the people of Israel. Early in Israel's history, the priest's ministry was centred upon the portable building known as the tabernacle, the construction of which is also described in the latter chapters of Exodus. In the time of the reign of King Solomon, hundreds of years later, the movable tabernacle was replaced with a permanent structure, the temple in Jerusalem, as detailed in 1 and 2 Kings. However, the layout and function of the temple and the tabernacle were exactly equivalent.

The temple was essentially a place of sacrifice, though it apparently served also as a place for prayer and teaching. Certainly by Jesus' time, rabbis taught on a regular basis in the courtyards that surrounded the temple. When Jesus overturned the tables of the money-changers and animal sellers, he did so in one of these courtyards, giving as his justification,

> "Is it not written, 'My house shall be called a house
> of prayer for all the nations?'" (Mark 11:17, quoting
> Isaiah 56:7)

Although prayer and teaching could take place in and around the temple, its chief function was to be a place of *sacrifice*. In some of these sacrifices, people would bring grain and even wine to offer to God, and these were presented to give thanks to God for his provision of their daily needs. Special sacrifices were also required at the end of the reaping of the crops, again as a harvest thanksgiving. The people could not, however, make these sacrifices themselves. They would give the materials for sacrifice to the priest and he would then make the sacrifices *on their behalf.* The grain would be burned on an open-air altar just outside the temple building, and the wine would be poured out on the ground near the altar, again by the priest *on their behalf.* God required a mediator.

Another group of offerings involved the sacrifice of certain animals to God. These were very serious sacrifices, and were always connected with the acknowledgement of guilt and the obtaining of forgiveness of sins from God. Underlying this process was an important principle in Scripture, summarized in Hebrews 9:22: "without the shedding of blood there is no forgiveness of sins".[1]

Why God should require the death of a substitute victim before people's sins can be forgiven is never fully explained in Scripture. The "Why does God…?" questions are always hard to respond to, as the final answers are usually locked up in heaven and inaccessible to us at this stage. It is sufficient to say that our sins must be far more serious in the sight of God than we can possibly imagine. Most of us think our failings are fairly trivial, especially when compared to those of other people we know, and especially when compared to the real monsters of history like Adolf Hitler or Pol Pot. Yet in the distressing example of Adam and Eve, it took just one seemingly insignificant sin to bring the

1. We may feel very squeamish about the idea of animals being killed as offerings, though, strangely, most of us have no problem with them being served up to us at dinnertime. Somehow the process seems more sanitized when straight from the supermarket!

full and terrible consequence of God's judgement upon them. Taking a forbidden piece of fruit does not rank very highly on our scale of sins when compared with, say, murder, adultery or genocide. We all probably commit worse failings every day of the week than Adam and Eve did. Most of us see ourselves as a sort of suburban sinner—better than Hitler but not as good as Mother Teresa! But the consequence for this one seemingly trivial sin was death and eviction from the presence of a God who apparently cannot tolerate sin in any form in which it may occur, however small in *our* eyes.

And so the Old Testament law, given by God himself, made provision for people to obtain the forgiveness of their sins, but only through the death of another life *on their behalf*.

Again, the people could not make these vital sacrifices by themselves. They were required by law to bring their offerings to the priests at the temple. Often whole families, including children, would attend and observe the process. The priest would accept the animal from their hands and it would be killed in front of them. The priests would collect some of the blood in vessels, and then pour the blood on parts of the altar and on the ground around it.

Part of what Israel was to learn from this process was that forgiveness of sins did not come cheaply. It was expensive for the family, who had to provide the best animal they could afford, and, of course, expensive for the poor animal. The number and types of sacrifices were very complex, and can be studied in the book of Leviticus.

Once a year there was a special national sacrifice on a day called the Day of Atonement. This was the most sacred day in the Jewish calendar, and the only day on which Israelites were expected to abstain from eating food. On this day and this day only, the high priest would take some of the blood of a sacrificed animal into the very temple building itself. He would go behind a large curtain into a secret and otherwise forbidden room called the 'Holy of Holies' or the 'Most Holy Place'. Here he would sprinkle the blood on the 'mercy seat' (a gold cover that rested on the famous 'ark of the covenant') and on the ground in front of it.

The primary function of an *hiereus*, therefore, was to act as a mediator between God and people, especially in the vital matter of obtaining the national forgiveness of sins.

To offer sacrifices at the altar on behalf of others was at the very heart of what it meant to be a priest.

Elder

A church leader in New Testament times was called *presbuteros*, nearly always translated 'elder' in English versions. A number of other words are used to describe this position of leader within the church, mainly *episkopos* ('overseer') and *poimenos* ('shepherd'). We have already seen that the New Testament writers use these three terms interchangeably, as in 1 Peter 5:1-2.

But—and this next point cannot be stressed too strongly— the word *hiereus* ('priest') is never, ever, used of a Christian church leader within the pages of the New Testament.

It is true, however, that the New Testament talks about *all* of God's people as a 'kingdom of priests', sometimes also referred to as the 'priesthood of all believers':

> You yourselves like living stones are being built up as a spiritual house, to be a holy priesthood, to offer spiritual sacrifices acceptable to God through Jesus Christ.
> (1 Pet 2:5)

How does this universal priesthood of the church work out in practice? Each of us, acting as a priest, is to offer a "living sacrifice" of ourselves to God through faith in Jesus Christ

(Rom 12:1-2). That is where we must start.

Suppose you have an opportunity to share your faith with another person. In sharing the gospel, you are acting as a mediator between God and that person. This is the method God has chosen by which the good news is to be passed on. In doing this mediatorial work, you are acting as a priest. If you pray for another person, you are acting as a mediator between that person and God. It is your priestly work. The New Testament spells out a variety of such spiritual sacrifices we may offer to God.

There are, therefore, two excellent reasons why the New Testament writers never use *hiereus* of an individual church leader, no matter how talented that person may be:

- To do so would be a denial of the high-priestly work of Christ, offering himself once for all in great love for us on the cross.
- To do so would be a denial of the priesthood of all believers, and would elevate one priest above all the other members of Christ.

Past its use-by date

As the early Christians, especially those living in and around Jerusalem, began to understand the full meaning of the death of Jesus upon the cross of Calvary, it became clear that the old sacrificial system was at an end. We would say today that it had passed its use-by date. The problem with the old system of sacrifices is that the sacrifices had to be offered over and over again. The system never worked perfectly, so the offerer could never say, "Well, I'll never have to do that again!" For nearly 1500 years before Jesus' time, rivers of blood had flowed at the hands of these human mediators between God and people. Every day, more and more sacrifices were offered.

Over a thousand times the high priest had gone once a year behind the curtain into the forbidden room to sprinkle sacrificial blood at the mercy seat. But it never worked perfectly. Next year he, or the new high priest, had to go back and do it all again.

The old system had three main elements:

- There had to be a priest to offer the sacrifice.
- There had to be a death so that the sacrifice could be offered.
- The sacrifice had to be as physically perfect as possible.

The early church came to understand, firstly through the teachings of Jesus himself and then through the additional revelations given to men like Paul, that the Jerusalem temple was functionally at an end:

- There had been a priest: Jesus himself.
- There had been the death of a sacrifice: Jesus himself.
- The sacrifice was the sinless, perfect, Son of God.

This is summed up most fully in the epistle to the Hebrews:

> But when Christ appeared as a *high priest* of the good things that have come, then through the greater and more perfect tent (not made with hands, that is, not of this creation) he entered *once for all* into the holy places, not by means of the blood of goats and calves but by means of his own *blood*, thus securing an eternal redemption. For if the blood of goats and bulls, and the sprinkling of defiled persons with the ashes of a heifer, sanctify for the purification of the flesh, how much more will the *blood of Christ*, who through the eternal Spirit offered himself *without blemish* to God, purify our conscience from dead works to serve the living God. (Heb 9:11-14)

The critical points here are:

- Christ is the high priest who is doing the offering.

- His offering is "once for all". Once performed, it is effective forever.
- Christ is the sacrifice, whose death has been offered.
- The offering is perfect in God's sight—"without blemish".

Notice also that the whole Trinity is involved in this perfect sacrifice:

> …how much more will the blood of *Christ*, who through the eternal *Spirit* offered himself without blemish to *God*…

It is Christ who offered himself. He did so by the power of the Spirit. The offering was made to God the Father.[2]

So you can see why the early church leaders never used *hiereus* in describing their role within the body of Christ. To do so would have been to discredit all that Christ had achieved by his Passion on the cross. The only mediator we need has accomplished his redemptive work by his death, once for all time, never to be repeated. The only ongoing mediator we need is already raised from the dead, seated at the Father's side. Paul stresses this:

> For there is one God, and there is one mediator between God and men, the man Christ Jesus, who gave himself as a ransom for all… (1 Tim 2:5-6)

And again, in the epistle to the Hebrews:

> Therefore [Christ] is the mediator of a new covenant…
> (Heb 9:15)

Why is this difference between the terms *hiereus* and *presbuteros*, as used in the New Testament, being so strongly stressed here? The reason is that as these two words have sailed through 2000

....

2. This is one of the few places in the New Testament that clearly state Jesus' sacrifice was made to God. In the Middle Ages, many taught and believed that he was offered to appease the Devil!

years of church history, they have become barnacle-encrusted, and their meanings have become intertwined, changed and muddied. Two critical historical periods illustrate this.

Confusion 1: 'priest' in the Middle Ages

The monk Jerome (c. 342-420 AD) translated the Bible from the original languages of Hebrew, Aramaic and Greek into the Latin tongue. This translation, known as the Vulgate, became the basis of the official Bible of the Roman Catholic Church. Until the time of the Reformation in the 16th century, it was the only Bible the faithful were allowed to read—provided they could read Latin, which most could not. Jerome correctly maintained the biblical distinction between *hiereus* and *presbuteros*. *Hiereus* he translated with the Latin word '*sacerdos*', and *presbuteros* he simply transliterated as '*presbyter*'.

Therefore, in the Roman Catholic Church, 'presbyter' remained as the basic term for a local church leader, and even today such a person lives in a house called the 'presbytery'.

But as Roman Catholic theology developed during the Middle Ages, the term 'presbyter' more and more began to take on the meaning of *hiereus* or 'priest'. There were two significant theological developments that formed the foundations for this gradual but radical change.

The first was the development of the doctrine of what is known by the somewhat cumbersome word 'transubstantiation' (literally, "a change of substance"). The church began to teach that in the Holy Communion, or Mass, as the priest utters the words of the service and especially the critical 'Prayer of Consecration', the bread and wine actually change into the physical body and blood of Jesus. The bread may still look, smell and taste like bread, but in reality it is the real body of Jesus, the church taught (and continues to teach). Likewise, the wine becomes the actual blood of Jesus. The substance of the elements changes, even though the 'accidents' or characteristics of taste, appearance and smell may remain the same. Only an officially ordained priest has the right and ability to petition God to perform this supernatural act. And because Jesus is now physically present, according to the church, the bread and wine can be worshipped by the faithful as God present with them.

This teaching then led to a second stage of development in the Mass, the doctrine of the sacrifice of the Mass. Once the elements of bread and wine have been changed into the actual body and blood of Christ, the priest then offers Jesus, really present, to God as a sacrifice for those attending the Mass. The Roman Catholic Church does not mean that Christ is sacrificed again in the Mass, it would appear, but rather that each Mass is a continuation of the sacrifice of Calvary. Although the meaning is not easy to establish, it is clear that the Mass is presented to God on behalf of the people as a sacrifice for sins—not only for those present but also for those already deceased. The table upon which this sacrifice is offered to God began to be called an 'altar', and to be constructed out of stone rather than wood. Priests began to wear special clothing said to have uniquely sacrificial significance. It was (and still is) only the properly ordained priest who could offer the sacrifice of the Mass. The church presbyter increasingly took on the role of essential mediator between God and the people. 'Presbyter' began more and more to look like *hiereus*.

Transubstantiation and the sacrifice of the Mass remain today the official central doctrines of the Roman Church. It is also interesting to note that Jerome, again in the Vulgate, used the Latin word *pontific* to translate 'high priest'. The head of the Catholic Church, the Pope, is still today referred to as the 'supreme Pontiff'.

Confusion 2: 'priest' during the English Reformation

After the death of King Henry VIII in the mid-16th century, reform of the church as a whole came to England. This work was headed up by the then Archbishop of Canterbury, Thomas Cranmer. Under his leadership, the church repudiated the twin doctrines of transubstantiation and the sacrifice of the Mass. In the Lord's Supper, or Holy Communion, the bread and wine do not change in substance, it was taught. (Cranmer and other leaders from this time would later pay for this repudiation with their lives in the fires of Oxford and Smithfield.) The Lord's Supper was to be held on a plain wooden table placed centrally in the body of the church. The officiating minister was to wear simpler clothes, and not stand with his back to the people, as if a mediator between them and God. The Lord's Supper was to be seen as basically a memorial of the once-for-all death that Jesus had offered to God. The bread and wine were to be eaten and drunk—not to be worshipped, which practice was described as a form of idolatry. If the faithful fed upon Christ in any way in this service, it was to be seen only as in a spiritual, not physical, manner.

The Bible was printed in English, and believers were encouraged to read it. People were taught that justification before God comes only through faith in the completed work of Jesus by his death, resurrection and ascension. Their good works could contribute nothing to the salvation won for them by their one and only mediator. And so the reforms kept coming.

Cranmer's most lasting legacy was the creation of the *Book of Common Prayer*, to be used throughout the newly reformed Church of England. In producing this Cranmer was in his element, and his Holy Communion service was a masterpiece of construction and the English tongue. Witness the opening words of this beautiful prayer, which Cranmer adapted from an ancient Spanish church service, to be said just before the reception of the bread and wine:

> We do not presume to come to this thy Table, O merciful Lord, trusting in our own righteousness, but in thy manifold and great mercies. We are not worthy so much as to gather up the crumbs under thy Table. But thou art the same Lord, whose property is always to have mercy.

But in the *Book of Common Prayer*, Cranmer retained the word 'priest' as the descriptive title for the officiating minister. Cranmer rightly understood that the English word 'priest' was simply a corruption of the Greek title 'presbyter', an elder in the local church. Although he was strictly correct in an etymological sense, I believe this was a tragic mistake. It is a well-established fact that languages are never static. The meanings of words change over time, and words can sometimes end up meaning something entirely different from their earlier sense. An often-quoted case is the word 'prevent', which to us means to stop something from happening, but in former times meant to precede or go ahead of another person. So the olden-day shepherd would 'prevent' the sheep, leading them from the front.

And so the word 'priest', during its progress through 1500 years of Roman Catholic theology, had picked up an additional meaning that it never had when it was the word *presbuteros* in the New Testament. 'Priest' had by this time become almost synonymous with the Greek word *hiereus*—a sacrificing mediator through whom you had to go if you wanted to have your sins forgiven and eventually reach heaven.

Many of the Christian leaders in England protested long and hard about Cranmer's retention of the title 'priest'. These became known collectively as the 'Puritans', as they felt that

Cranmer's reforms had not gone far enough and were not 'pure' enough. Some stayed within the Church of England while many, including John Bunyan and the American Pilgrim Fathers, eventually left and formed dissenting congregations.

Most non-Catholic congregations today prefer to use 'pastor', 'elder' or even 'minister' to describe the person who has leadership within the congregation. The retention of the title 'priest' by much of the Anglican Communion continues, I believe, to cause confusion in the minds of many people. It is interesting to note that parts of this communion have ceased to use the word. From a biblical standpoint, they seem to have a good case.

Feedback on this resource

We really appreciate getting feedback about our resources— not just suggestions for how to improve them, but also positive feedback and ways they can be used. We especially love to hear that the resources may have helped someone in their Christian growth.

You can send feedback to us via the 'Feedback' menu in our online store, or write to us at PO Box 225, Kingsford NSW 2032, Australia.

matthiasmedia

Matthias Media is an evangelical publishing ministry that seeks to persuade all Christians of the truth of God's purposes in Jesus Christ as revealed in the Bible, and equip them with high-quality resources, so that by the work of the Holy Spirit they will:

- abandon their lives to the honour and service of Christ in daily holiness and decision-making
- pray constantly in Christ's name for the fruitfulness and growth of his gospel
- speak the Bible's life-changing word whenever and however they can—in the home, in the world and in the fellowship of his people.

It was in 1988 that we first started pursuing this mission, and in God's kindness we now have more than 300 different ministry resources being used all over the world. These resources range from Bible studies and books through to training courses and audio sermons.

To find out more about our large range of very useful resources, and to access samples and free downloads, visit our website:

www.matthiasmedia.com

How to buy our resources

1. Direct from us over the internet:
   - in the US: www.matthiasmedia.com
   - in Australia and the rest of the world: www.matthiasmedia.com.au

2. Direct from us by phone:
   - in the US: 1 866 407 4530
   - in Australia: 1300 051 220
   - international: +61 2 9233 4627

> Register at our website for our **free** regular email update to receive information about the latest new resources, **exclusive special offers**, and free articles to help you grow in your Christian life and ministry.

3. Through a range of outlets in various parts of the world. Visit **www.matthiasmedia.com/contact** for details about recommended retailers in your part of the world, including www.thegoodbook.co.uk in the United Kingdom.

4. Trade enquiries can be addressed to:
   - in the US and Canada: sales@matthiasmedia.com
   - in Australia and the rest of the world: sales@matthiasmedia.com.au

The Trellis and the Vine

by Colin Marshall and Tony Payne

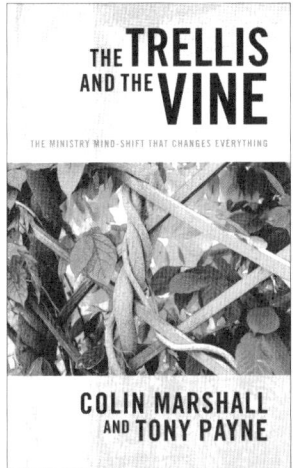

All Christian ministry is a mixture of trellis and vine.

There is vine work: the prayerful preaching and teaching of the word of God to see people converted and grow to maturity as disciples of Christ. And there is trellis work: creating and maintaining the physical and organizational structures and programs that support vine work and its growth.

What's the state of the trellis and the vine in your part of the world? Has trellis work taken over, as it has a habit of doing? Is the vine work being done by very few (perhaps only the pastor and only on Sundays)? And is the vine starting to wilt as a result?

In *The Trellis and the Vine*, Colin Marshall and Tony Payne answer afresh urgent fundamental questions about Christian ministry. They dig back into the Bible's view of Christian ministry, and argue that a major mind-shift is required if we are to fulfill the Great Commission of Christ, and see the vine flourish again.

FOR MORE INFORMATION OR TO ORDER CONTACT:

Matthias Media
Ph: 1300 051 220
Int: +61 2 9233 4627
Email: sales@matthiasmedia.com.au
www.matthiasmedia.com.au

Matthias Media (USA)
Ph: 1 866 407 4530
Int: +1 330 953 1702
Email: sales@matthiasmedia.com
www.matthiasmedia.com